The
Public
Relations
Audit

Evaluation Checklists to Measure the
Impact of Every Message You Send to
Customers, Shareholders and the Public

Norman Hart
Norman Hart Associates

FINANCIAL TIMES
Prentice Hall

An imprint of **PEARSON EDUCATION**

London • New York • San Francisco • Toronto • Sydney
Tokyo • Singapore • Hong Kong • Cape Town • Madrid • Paris • Milan • Munich • Amsterdam

PEARSON EDUCATION LIMITED

Head Office:
Edinburgh Gate
Harlow CM20 2JE
Tel: +44 (0)1279 623623
Fax: +44 (0)1279 431059

London Office:
128 Long Acre, London WC2E 9AN
Tel: +44 (0)207 447 2000
Fax: +44 (0)207 240 5771
Website: www.business-minds.com

First published in Great Britain in 2000

© Cambridge Strategy Publications Ltd 2000

Published in association with
Cambridge Strategy Publications Ltd
39 Cambridge Place
Cambridge CB2 1NS

The right of Norman Hart to be identified as Author
of this Work has been asserted by him in accordance
with the Copyright, Design and Patents Act 1988.

ISBN 0 273 64939 6

British Library Cataloguing in Publication Data
A CIP catalogue record for this book can be obtained from the British Library

10 9 8 7 6 5 4 3 2 1

Typeset by Pantek Arts, Maidstone, Kent
Printed and bound in Great Britain

The Publishers' policy is to use paper manufactured from sustainable forests.

CONTENTS

Part 1: The Public Relations Audit 1

Introduction 3

What Are We Doing Now? 11

Step 1: The Internal Image Audit 13

Step 2: The Consultancy Audit 23

Step 3: Choosing a Consultancy 27

Step 4: Assessing Staff Skills and Competencies 29

Step 5: Public Relations Publics Audit 35

Step 6: Selecting the Media 39

Step 7: Good Media Relations 47

Step 8: Public Relations Evaluation 51

Step 9: The Ten-Point Public Relations Plan 53

Checklists 57

Part 2: The Audit Process 59

Staffing the Audit Team 61

Creating an Audit Project Plan 63

Laying the Groundwork for the Audit 65

Analyzing Audit Results 67

Sharing Audit Results 71

Writing Effective Audit Reports 73

Dealing with Resistance to Recommendations .77

Building an Ongoing Audit Program 81

Part 3: Implementing a Public Relations Audit: Questions and Checklists 83

Step 1: The Internal Image Audit 85

Step 2: The Consultancy Audit 91

Step 3: Choosing a Consultancy 93

Step 4: Assessing Staff Skills and Competencies 97

Step 5: Public Relations Publics Audit 99

Step 6: Selecting the Media 103

Step 7: Good Media Relations 111

Step 8: Public Relations Evaluation 115

Step 9: The Ten-Point Public Relations Plan 117

THE PUBLIC RELATIONS AUDIT

This audit is structured in three parts. Part 1 examines the process of carrying out a public relations audit. Part 2 looks at the audit process itself and provides a framework that addresses some of the logistical and process requirements of conducting an audit. Part 3 comprises a series of questions based on the steps in Part 1. These questions are designed to help you plan and implement your audit in a straightforward and practical manner.

INTRODUCTION

What Is Public Relations?

There are many misconceptions as to what exactly is meant by public relations or, as it is more popularly and misleadingly known, PR. The general public regards it as a deliberate effort to obscure the truth, and to put up a favorable screen around the organization or person concerned. 'It's just a PR stunt' means simply it is propaganda, or even lies. The understanding of public relations is not a great deal better in much of business and commerce where the abbreviation is taken to refer to 'press relations', i.e. obtaining free editorial publicity in the press and other media. And if this means a program of activities to catch the media's attention, then this is a public relations program.

True public relations, however, is something quite different, and simply put is the *establishment*, *maintenance* and *enhancement* of an organization's reputation. The fact is, of course, all organizations have public relations whether they like it or not. Sending out no messages at all communicates a message in itself. The only issue to be considered is whether or not to 'manage' one's public relations. Done properly, it comprises a deliberate and planned system of communications between an organization and its publics in order to project a favorable corporate image, sometimes referred to as reputation or goodwill. The outcome of public relations has a value, and sometimes a very high one at that.

The 'publics' referred to are all those discrete groups of people whose support is important to the organization's betterment. The term 'stakeholders' is increasingly used, and covers such groups as:

• shareholders

• potential shareholders

• financial analysts and advisers

• stockbrokers and institutions

• banks and accountancy practices

• employees, past, present and future

• trade unions and employers' bodies

• customers and prospects

• distributors

• government—local, national and international

• local communities

• opinion formers and pressure groups.

An important point to note, right at the outset, is nowhere in the definition does it say 'by means of press publicity or media relations'. The channels of communication used in public relations are those which, for a given campaign, are the most cost effective. Editorial publicity is widely employed simply because it is the most cost-effective medium, but the largest item in many public relations budgets is advertising.

Public relations must have as its ultimate goal the support of, and contribution towards, the achievement of the organization's objectives. In a profit-making business, the public relations activity must increase profit. With non-commercial bodies or professional institutions, the objectives might be social ones, attracting membership, raising educational standards, attracting charitable donations, or any of a number of goals.

The role of public relations is proving to be even more necessary in services since, in the absence of tangible products, there is a need for even stronger perceptions.

Strategic Public Relations

Not only must public relations be aimed at an organization's strategic objectives, the very operation itself is strategic as exemplified by its application to the various business functions such as finance, human resources and marketing.

With finance, for instance, it intrinsically affects the worth of a commercial enterprise whether it likes it or not. The determination of share prices is obviously by return on investment, both actual and forecast. But also of importance is what might be termed the 'risk factor'. Just how safe does a potential investor feel about a given company? And what is felt about its long-term growth? As confidence in a company grows, so does its share value. This, in turn, also has the effect of keeping predators at bay and reducing the likelihood of a takeover.

On the human resources side of a business, good public relations has a strategic effect on whether or not people will want to work for an organization. In recruitment advertising, for instance, the ingredients of an advertisement will include a number of tactical incentives, such as salary, job title, car, and pension. The strategic element is simply the organization's reputation. As this increases, so do the number of applicants, from which a higher-quality person will be employed. Long term (strategically), this strengthens the quality of the workforce, and perhaps even more importantly increases morale and motivation, since everyone likes to work for an employer who is well regarded. The outcome is higher efficiency and effectiveness coupled with a lower employee turnover.

For many firms, the function most readily benefiting from public relations activities is marketing where a strong reputation, regardless of benefits offered by the product or service, increases the propensity to buy. Public relations brings together an emerging, highly profitable combination of corporate image and brand image, as explained below.

Public Relations and Marketing

In the US marketing communications are broken down into four specific areas. There is advertising for products and services—all those activities which can be classified as 'above-the-line'. Then there is sales promotion, largely 'below-the-line' media. Next comes the salesforce and all personal, face-to-face communications. Finally, there is 'publicity', referring to free editorial publicity and all the various activities involved in generating it. Public relations is not seen as part of marketing, but product editorial publicity certainly is.

Marketing versus public relations

Just as the old chestnut of advertising versus public relations continues to be debated, so does the question of whether public relations should be part of marketing. The fact is advertising is just one of a number of channels of communication available to promote a product (and thus a subset of marketing), or to promote an organization (and thus a subset of public relations). Equally, editorial publicity can contribute powerfully to product promotion (marketing) or corporate promotion (public relations).

The simplest way of expressing the difference is to discriminate between brand or product image, and corporate or company image. This difference then resolves itself nicely into tactical matters and strategic. Product promotion has, of course, long-term objectives, but many actions are with the short term in mind. Price changes, distribution, packaging, presentation, advertising—all are used to generate sales or maybe sales leads. The focus is the product. The supporting strategic element is the image or reputation of the company promoting the product.

What public relations does for marketing is to create a favorable atmosphere around a product, i.e. it increases the propensity to buy.

More companies use public relations in marketing

A company can choose whether to develop and promote a brand image, a corporate image, or both. Many companies have done well enough by having only a brand image, e.g. Unilever and Procter & Gamble. But then they have other problems centering around having competing brands whose credibility would be undermined if there was a common corporate image in the product promotion.

Other companies have the very opposite—a corporate image and no brand image, e.g. most Japanese consumer durables. Some products, on the other hand, have always had both, e.g. cars. A buyer of a Fiesta car in the UK must also feel comfortable with Ford as the organization behind it. Nowadays, however, more and more companies are waking up to the extra competitive edge to be obtained from having a corporate image to support brand image. One of the major changes in recent times, for example, has been with Cadbury, whose products like Wispa, Crunchie, Dairy Milk, and Milk Tray all now have a corporate identity. A similar development has occurred with Rowntree Mackintosh, now part of Nestlé, in relation to Polo mints and Black Magic chocolates.

Five dependent marketing variables

Whether or not a product is purchased depends on five factors and not four (the 4Ps)—namely, the product, its price, its availability (place), the brand image (promotion), and the corporate image, if any. Each one of these variables can act in a positive or negative way, but the net effect must obviously be positive for a purchase to take place.

Thus, in Figure 1, a product might be very good (positive) but the price rather high (negative). The brand name might be unknown (neutral) but the manufacturer highly regarded (positive). The product benefits and corporate image, in this case, must clearly be strong enough to overcome the 'price', 'place' and 'brand image' barriers. The attractiveness of the total product offering demonstrates both the polarity of each factor (positive or negative) and its intensity. A series of such diagrams facilitates comparison of all competitive products in a market segment, and highlights their strengths and weaknesses.

Such an analysis enables a strategy to be selected for increasing market share of one's own product simply by considering which one (or more) of the five factors is likely to be the most cost effective in beating the competition.

Alternatively, one can look at a constant market share but trade off one factor against another, for example the price could be increased but corporate image strengthened without loss of sales. In so far as public relations is the function building reputation or corporate image, it can be seen to have a direct correlation with sales and hence

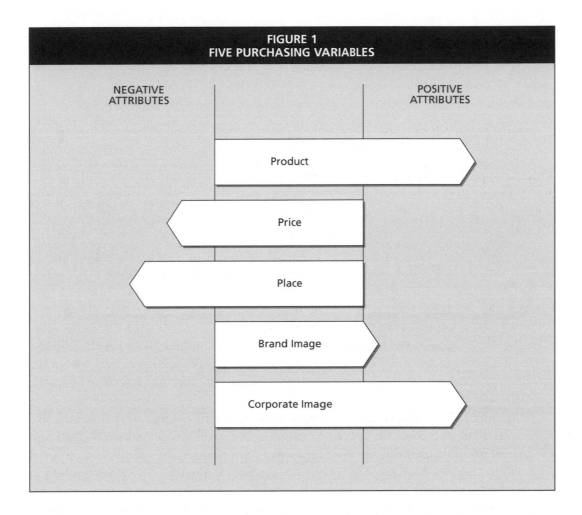

**FIGURE 1
FIVE PURCHASING VARIABLES**

NEGATIVE ATTRIBUTES

POSITIVE ATTRIBUTES

Product

Price

Place

Brand Image

Corporate Image

with profit. It is a real investment which can be, and is, expressed in financial terms, such as 'goodwill'.

The marketing function

Figure 2 illustrates the principal marketing functions, all aimed primarily at customers and prospects. The non face-to-face elements are shown as breaking down into the various channels of communication, such as advertising, publicity (editorials), direct mail, exhibitions, and so on. There is a comprehensive, and hopefully synergistic, marketing communications plan which, together with a similar sales plan, goes to make up the promotion element of the 4Ps. Public relations does not come into this since it is, by definition, concerned with the reputation or image of the organization behind the product.

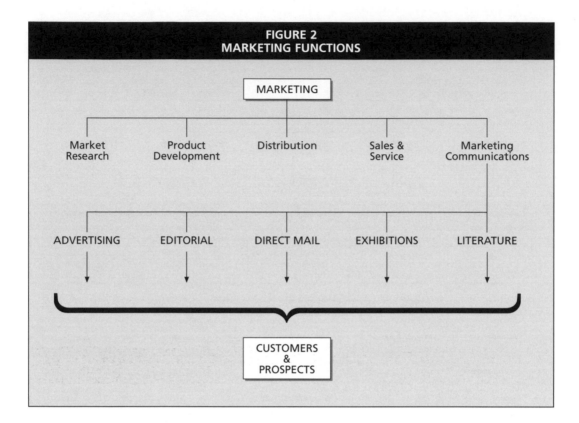

The public relations function

Figure 3 bears a remarkable resemblance to the previous figure, except the number of target audiences has been increased to cover, in effect, all the 'stakeholders' of a business. Thus, the appropriate messages are sent out to employees, shareholders, pressure groups, and so on, but using precisely the same channels of communication as in the case of marketing. Certainly, editorial publicity figures high on the list but, equally, consideration must be given to advertising where publicity alone cannot achieve the public relations objectives.

Relationship between marketing and public relations

A block schematic diagram, as shown in Figure 4, indicates the relationship between marketing and public relations. Public relations starts with a state of unawareness among its various publics including, of course, customers and prospects. It takes them through being aware of a company and on to a perception which, of course, needs to be positive. Similarly, marketing is concerned with moving a prospect from unawareness of the product to awareness, and on to a favorable perception.

The two streams come together with the establishment of 'behavioral intent'. But here, and in subsequent stages, three other factors come into play which might render

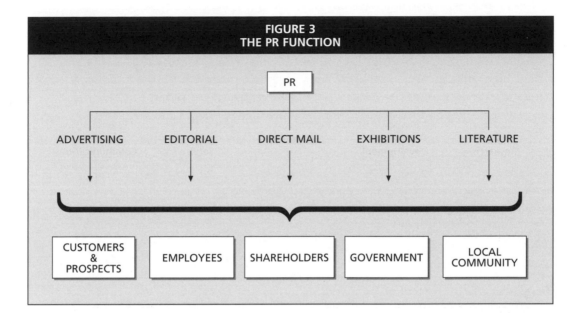

FIGURE 3
THE PR FUNCTION

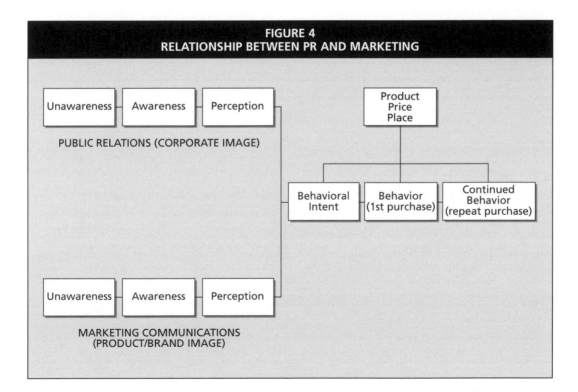

FIGURE 4
RELATIONSHIP BETWEEN PR AND MARKETING

all the communications in the world useless in terms of subsequent sales. These are the remaining 3Ps, product, price and place. If the price is too high, for example, then the product will not be purchased (behavior), or even considered (behavioral intent), let alone continue to be purchased.

Summary

Public relations throughout the world is beginning to be recognized as a new and independent management function, quite separate to marketing. It is essentially strategic, and contributes to overall business objectives by providing effective communications channels to assist all the other management functions.

WHAT ARE WE DOING NOW?

There is frequently some confusion between *corporate image* and *corporate identity* and, for that matter, *corporate culture*. Corporate image has already been discussed, and in broad terms can be said to be the perception people have about an organization, not about a product, which is *product* or *brand image*. The matter is further confused by the use of the term *corporate brand*. This, however, should be regarded as a synonym of corporate image. *Corporate identity* (ID) comprises all those factors which, together, combine to create a corporate image. It is frequently restricted to cover just the graphics and symbolism relating to an organization. This takes in letterheads and the like, typography, logos, corporate colors, and so on. There is, of course, much more to it, and this will be discussed in some detail below. As for corporate culture, this is also an important contributing factor to corporate image, and is simply the way in which people behave within the confines of a particular organization.

THE INTERNAL IMAGE AUDIT

O ver the past few years, a new way of examining an organization's image has been developed. This has been based on a broader view of all the factors leading to the creation of image.

The starting point is obviously to appraise all the deliberate and active sources of publicity such as advertising, direct mail, exhibitions, and so on. An advertisement, for instance, will have a specific purpose, maybe to generate inquiries for a particular product or service. Whether it is successful or not might depend on the number of inquiries produced compared with the objective. This, however, overlooks another important role performed by any advertisement, the impression it creates of the organization behind it. A small advertisement tucked away at the back of a publication might pull in inquiries but give an impression of being a minor business compared to its competitors. Equally, a large and lavish advertisement might give the impression of a business not too careful with its money, of having more money than sense. So, every *active message source* should be evaluated in terms of: 'What impression will it create?'

In the field of marketing there are many other message sources, some far more important. The single most influential factor on whether someone buys a product is what can be termed third-party endorsement, i.e. recommendation by a buyer or user of the product.

But not just people outside the organization affect what people think of it. What impression is given, for instance, when the chief executive makes a speech: good or bad? And what about the telephonist, or a secretary, or the salesforce? Specific groups of people should be identified and evaluated to see where there could be changes to improve the impressions being created.

A final roundup brings in what are referred to as *passive message sources*. These comprise any factor in any way contributing to public perception. The appearance of the offices and reception, for instance, coupled with the way visitors are greeted; the tidiness of the office desks, job titles, letter headings, vehicles, etc.—the list is endless. One of the great attractions of conducting such a comprehensive review of message sources is, in many instances, changes can take place quickly and without any great expense.

TABLE 1

ACTIVE MESSAGE SOURCES (PROMOTIONAL)

1. Press advertising
2. TV
3. Radio
4. Outdoor
5. Public exhibitions
6. Private exhibitions
7. Films, video and AV
8. Demonstrations and visits
9. Sponsorship
10. Telemarketing
11. Sales leaflets and brochures
12. Business gifts
13. Directories and yearbooks
14. Educational packs
15. Sales calls
16. Merchandising
17. Point of sale
18. Sales promotion
19. Envelope franking, letter stuffers and stickers, etc.
20. Sales aids
21. Direct mail
22. Seminars and conferences
23. Press releases
24. Press receptions
25. Press visits
26. Government and other lobbies
27. Charity support
28. Feature articles

OUTSIDE MESSAGE SOURCES

29. Agents and distributors
30. Customers—specifiers, authorizers, purchasers
31. Users
32. Journalists
33. Trade associations
34. Consultants
35. Local community
36. Competitors
37. Suppliers

PEOPLE MESSAGE SOURCES

38. Company VIPs
39. Sales force
40. Service engineers
41. Telephonist
42. Receptionist
43. Employees in general
44. Spouses and friends
45. Shareholders
46. Applications for jobs
47. Handling complaints
48. Membership of trade associations
49. Membership of learned institutes
50. Attendance at conferences
51. Chairing committees
52. Public speaking
53. Local community activities
54. Social activities

PASSIVE MESSAGE SOURCES

55. Annual report
56. Sales letters
57. Company name
58. House magazine/newsletters
59. Sales office backup
60. House style
61. Packaging
62. Labels
63. Telephone contact
64. Business cards
65. Specification sheets
66. Test certificates
67. Instruction manuals
68. Service manuals
69. Delivery notes and invoices
70. Cars, delivery vehicles
71. Price list/credit facilities
72. Pre-sales service
73. Christmas cards
74. Telex
75. Facsimile messages
76. Telephone directory entries
77. Trademark
78. Calendars
79. Diaries
80. Wall charts
81. Photographs
82. Showrooms
83. Appearance of factory
84. Location
85. Ties and emblems
86. Brand names
87. Logotypes
88. Royal Warrant
89. Queen's Award to Industry
90. Reception area
91. Noticeboards
92. The product—quality, appearance, etc
93. Delivery promises—reliability
94. Group name
95. Nationality
96. Range of product/application
97. Warranty cards/trading terms
98. Samples
99. Job titles
100. Visitors/entertaining

The starting point is to produce a checklist of message sources to be used for the audit. Then a small project team of, say, three senior people needs to be assembled with a view to reaching a consensus on whether any given message source is creating a favorable, neutral, or unfavorable impression. The objective is to create a list of all message sources obviously in the unfavorable category, with a view to setting in motion an action program. Stage two is to examine the neutral message sources, and, finally, can those already favorable be made even more favorable?

The External Image Audit

Many of the message sources listed above will be seen in the same way by people within an organization as by those outside it. For this reason, the first step is to conduct an internal image audit. Having done this, however, it is prudent to run through the same procedure with a group of people from outside, typically with customers. A customer panel may be considered adequate, though statistically it cannot be relied on. Some important message sources may also have been missed, if the list was drawn up only by inside staff. To overcome this, a useful technique is to resort initially to a focus group discussion which might uncover some further criteria to be added to the audit.

At this stage, it may be necessary to engage the services of an outside market research company and, where considerable doubt is uncovered about the current perception of any of the message sources, to extend the study to quantitative research.

The Corporate Personality

In any study of corporate image we must be absolutely clear about what image is required. This might come out of the *mission statement*, but simply expressed it can be regarded as the *corporate personality*. It is the impression springing to mind whenever the company name is mentioned. And this is not simply a question of a good or bad image. It must be refined to project the nature of the business. A few examples will serve to indicate the attributes potentially associated with a company name:

- innovative, proactive, creative

- market leader, profitable

- well managed, reliable, safe, responsible

- international, British, Japanese, or any other nationality

- diversified, specialist

- authoritative, technical leader, expert

- honest, decent, truthful

• high quality, value for money

• friendly, responsive, caring

• excellent in pre- and post-sales service.

Organizing for Public Relations

The first, and most important, step in organizing for public relations is to position it correctly within the management structure. It is common practice to have public relations reporting to the marketing director, if there is one, or even the sales director or, alternatively, to the company secretary.

Figure 5 shows how the public relations function currently fits in with other management functions. The left-hand box takes in the *formulation* of business or corporate objectives, and the strategies needed to achieve them. Here, the managing director or chief executive will play a leading part and will be supported by all the other main board directors, such as finance, human resources, production, and so on.

A move to the right takes us on from *implementation* to *execution*, and each of the functional directors takes the relevant business strategy (e.g. to contribute to the business objective—profit—by means of a cost-cutting exercise—a financial strategy) which now becomes a tactical financial objective. And so functional plans are constructed for each of the major business strategies. There is a marketing plan, a financial plan, and so on. The exception to this can be seen to be the public relations

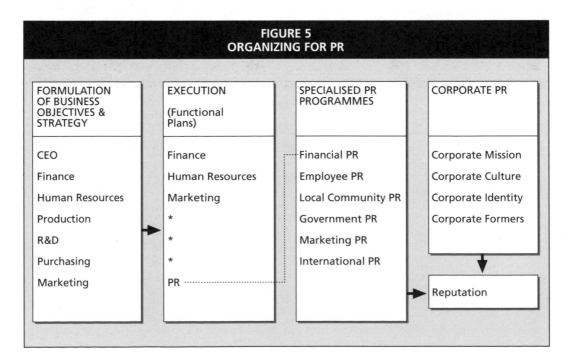

FIGURE 5
ORGANIZING FOR PR

FORMULATION OF BUSINESS OBJECTIVES & STRATEGY	EXECUTION (Functional Plans)	SPECIALISED PR PROGRAMMES	CORPORATE PR
CEO	Finance	Financial PR	Corporate Mission
Finance	Human Resources	Employee PR	Corporate Culture
Human Resources	Marketing	Local Community PR	Corporate Identity
Production	*	Government PR	Corporate Formers
R&D	*	Marketing PR	
Purchasing	*	International PR	
Marketing	PR		Reputation

plan. Obviously such a plan is required, but top management thinking does not include either how public relations should be contributing to business objectives, or to what extent the business objectives require public relations activities to be achieved.

Just to complete the picture of how the various components of a public relations program fit together, the next box shows a number of specialized programs each giving support to and collaborating with another management function, and resulting in an integrated, and hopefully synergistic, activity leading on to the maintenance and development of corporate image or reputation. Moving on to the right-hand box, a number of corporate activities will also make a contribution to reputation, i.e. the *corporate mission*, the *corporate culture*, and the *corporate identity*. Corporate mission simply means 'what we are and what we aim to do, our unique ethical stance and strategic objectives'.

The overall conclusion is the public relations function should report directly to the CEO, and the executive concerned should be given the same status as the other functional heads with whom he or she will have to deal. The still common practice of being part of the marketing team is not good enough. True, public relations has an important contribution to make to marketing, but it is also making contributions to finance, human resources and, indeed, the business as a whole.

Internal/External Services

One growing issue is to what extent various specialized functions should be outsourced. Business communications covers a very wide range of activities with an equally wide range of outside services from which to choose. Table 2 indicates some of them.

TABLE 2 OUTSIDE SERVICES
<table><tr><td>• Agencies</td><td>• Audiovisual producers</td></tr><tr><td>• Writers</td><td>• Exhibition/display</td></tr><tr><td>• Graphic designers</td><td>• Marketing consultancy</td></tr><tr><td>• Media brokers</td><td>• Photographers</td></tr><tr><td>• Public relations consultants</td><td>• Photographic/model agencies</td></tr><tr><td>• Public relations distributors</td><td>• Conference organizers</td></tr><tr><td>• Direct mail houses</td><td>• Translation services</td></tr><tr><td>• List brokers</td><td>• Sales promotion agencies</td></tr><tr><td>• Market research companies</td><td>• Merchandising agencies</td></tr><tr><td>• Telephone marketing</td><td>• Recruitment agencies</td></tr><tr><td>• Total communications</td><td>• Training organizations</td></tr><tr><td>• Printers</td><td></td></tr></table>

Obviously the most important outside service within the context of a public relations operation is the public relations consultancy itself.

Should an organization make use of a public relations consultancy? Over the past decade, the use of outside consultancies has grown from a very small, and perhaps dubious, base to something of the order of 50 percent (compared with advertising agency usage of around 90 percent).

Strengths

Professional. It is only reasonable to expect consultants to bring to bear much more professional expertise than any in-house person. After all, they will probably have been in their particular specialism most of their working lives. They are working full time on several clients at the same time, and with a number of colleagues whose experience is also available.

Objectivity. An outside person can contribute an objective point of view, unimpeded by tradition and past practice, corporate culture ('that is the way we do things here'), personal influence, or any subjectivity. This alternative input may happen to be the right one, and otherwise might have been missed, or even dismissed.

Credibility. It might seem to be a strange factor to put forward as a strength, but very often the opinion of an outside consultant will be accepted, even though precisely the same point was rejected when put by an in-house person.

Expandable service. Consultancy services can be purchased in small increments whereas with an in-house appointment one has to have a whole person (unless sharing a function). Going to the other extreme, a very large service can be obtained, at relatively short notice, and subsequently discontinued without any problem. The variations in communication needs are never level and constant, and so there is considerable value in having at least part of the 'supply' side capable of expansion and contraction whenever required.

Weaknesses

Limited time. An outside consultancy has a number of other clients to look after, and from time to time they are going to be given priority, or simply get in the way. Each member of a consultancy is limited in the time allocated to any one account by the fee being paid by the particular client. All consultants keep time sheets on which their hours are recorded in exactly the same way as, say, an accountancy practice. In contrast, a staff member is likely to be instantly available and will work on a job until it is complete without any question of how it is going to be paid for.

Superficial. Any outside person lacks the kind of personal involvement a staff member has. As a result, the work done often appears to be superficial, to lack depth and, therefore, credibility. This is particularly so with any product or service which is technical or in some way complex, e.g. with IT work or, say, personal pension schemes.

Expensive. It is a useful exercise for any organization contemplating the use of a public relations consultancy to check the charge-out rate for the various executives who are likely to be working on the account. These could well be anything up to ten times the cost of an equivalent in-house person. Other financial factors to investigate are daily rates, monthly fees (particularly the minimum acceptable or, indeed, desirable), the extras to be paid for, and the method of charging up on suppliers' invoices before being passed on. Two 'rules of thumb' here are: the overall cost of a very modest public relations campaign is likely to be double the fee charged; and the common uplift given to a supplier's invoice is 17.65 percent, which rather illogically equates to the equivalent 15 percent media commission obtained by an advertising agency in respect of clients' billings.

Staff turnover. Public relations services are growing and there is never a sufficient supply of competent staff to meet the need. The really good staff are continually being tempted away to a more attractive and better paid position. The additional payment is borne ultimately by the client. A typical length of stay for a public relations executive is two years which, in some cases, is hardly enough time to get a first grasp of the job to be done.

When, if and why

There are a range of options to be considered, starting at doing all the public relations operations in-house and finishing with putting the whole lot out. At the very least any organization, no matter how small, can benefit from outside advice, if only on setting down the objectives together with a plan of action to achieve them. This need not be at all an expensive operation. Certain parts of the plan's implementation may be better handled in-house, say, routine press releases, whereas special projects, such as a major conference or parliamentary relations, require special expertise which has to come from outside. On this issue, two very simple steps can be taken without too much in the way of cost, time and trouble. These are to write down comprehensively the activities which need to be undertaken in order to achieve the public relations objectives, whether done inside or outside. The second step is to talk with one or two consultancies in order to find out in what ways they would feel able to contribute. The procedure for choosing a consultancy is dealt with in some detail later in this audit.

Using and Auditing a Consultancy

Consultancy fees are increasing, resulting in an understandable pressure to obtain good value for money and an unwillingness to accept anything other than first-class service and performance. This has led to a review of relationships and procedures in which two factors have emerged. First, the consultancy must receive from the client all the necessary information required in order to do a first-class job, i.e. an adequate briefing. Secondly, there must be a method of evaluating the service provided, i.e. an audit.

Briefing

Within the sometimes fragile relationship between a consultancy and a client, there must always be the possibility of either party's performance needing to be improved. Thus, before a client starts to criticize its consultancy, it must be confident it has done everything possible to enable the consultancy to perform outstandingly well. This must be achieved by, in the first place, ensuring all the personnel who will have any involvement with the account are thoroughly familiar with the nature of the client's business, its products and markets, and its objectives. This should be achieved by what can be termed a *background brief*. Over and above this, however, for every job undertaken the individual briefing must also be thorough in every way. This might be referred to as the *tactical brief*. Only when these actions have been taken can the consultancy be reasonably criticized.

The background brief

All the people likely to be working on the account need to be sufficiently well informed to be able to pick up a job with only the minimum of briefing, and to complete the assignment to a high standard and in the shortest of time, certainly without any revisions let alone rejections. Initially, a one- or two-day seminar may be convened with senior specialists from the client company attending to put across their particular function. The following topics should be included. Much of the information will be of a confidential and sensitive nature. However, this is necessary if the two groups are going to work together efficiently and in harmony.

Objectives. The short- and long-term objectives for the business (profit?), marketing (market share), sales (products and territories), finance, human resources, research and development, and any others.

External factors. Anticipated factors outside the control of the company which may affect whether it achieves its objectives. These can conveniently be pinpointed by a PEEST analysis—Political, Economic, Environmental, Sociological and Technological.

Internal factors. These come very well out of the classical SWOT analysis—Strengths, Weaknesses, Opportunities and Threats.

The market. Knowledge of market size, perceptions and motivation.

Product portfolio. Familiarity with the entire range of products, their attributes and the benefits they offer.

Competition. How all the competitors match up to the client's own products.

Pricing strategy. The basis of pricing and the relationship with competitive prices.

Service. Pre-sales, sales and post-sales service.

The above list is heavily marketing biased and should be seen as indicative of the background knowledge which will assist a public relations executive to produce good first-time work for a client. Each individual organization must produce a menu, as above, of the most helpful areas of interest and, having done this in the first instance, must then make provision for a periodic update.

The tactical brief

The only safe and adequate way of providing a brief for the consultancy is to set it down in writing and ensure before it is handed over it has the approval of any senior management who will wish to have a say in the final outcome, e.g. in approving a press release.

THE CONSULTANCY AUDIT

One of the most elusive factors in the whole communications process is finding some effective means of assessing a public relations consultancy's performance. A tried and tested method is to set up a structured annual consultancy audit giving an immediate measure in absolute terms as well as providing an excellent benchmark for measuring change in the level of client satisfaction.

The key to setting up an audit is to draw up a list of, say, 10 criteria against which the consultancy's performance is to be judged. This will naturally vary from one client company to another, as will the particular importance of each item.

The criteria then form the basis of an annual review meeting in which the client gives an assessment of the extent to which the consultancy has provided the service required. This can be simply against a semantic rating, e.g. 'very good', 'average' or 'completely unacceptable', or it can be against arithmetical ratings in which a mark is allocated against a total possible score.

The format is very simple, quick and, most importantly, inexpensive. A meeting is set up in which the key people from both consultancy and client come together to give a frank exchange of views. Against the client's appraisal, the consultancy will have the opportunity to give explanations, and agreement can be reached on a course of action.

This process should not be seen as a preamble to the consultancy being fired; quite the opposite. By highlighting dissatisfactions before they reach a critical stage it is, at the very least, a way of avoiding such terminal action. Indeed, the audit should be seen as a way of applauding good service and of giving credit when it is due.

Below is a checklist on the whole range of services. Each in turn can be examined in order to identify the need for change, if any, and to pinpoint areas of satisfaction and dissatisfaction.

The figures on the right-hand side are given as a guide to quantifying the audit by allocating marks of satisfaction against a possible weighting. They will obviously vary from client to client, but they have been chosen such that the total possible ratings add up to 100. Thus, the allocated ratings when summed represent a percentage in which 100 percent indicates complete satisfaction, and any lower score provides a measure of dissatisfaction with an immediate indication of where remedial action is required.

Consultancy Audit Checklist

Services	Satisfaction rating
1. Basis of remuneration	☐ (5)
2. Methods of costing and charging, allocation of overheads	☐ (10)
3. Knowledge of relevant industries and markets	☐ (10)
4. Quality of press releases or other specific activities in relation to brief of: (a) Copywriting (b) Headline (c) Action (d) Visuals or photography (e) Campaign continuity (f) Measurement of results	☐ (15)
5. Campaign assessment in relation of brief of: (a) Campaign plan (b) Media mix (c) Continuity (d) Measurement of results	☐ (15)
6. Media services and expertise (planning and buying) in: (a) Press (b) TV (c) Radio (d) Press conferences (e) Press visits	☐ (15)

(f) Literature
(g) Technical publications
(h) Private exhibitions
(i) Trade shows
(j) Photography
(k) Road shows
(l) Audio
(m) Video

7. Research ☐ (5)
   (a) Awareness
   (b) Editorial publicity
   (c) Media
   (d) Attitude
   (e) Campaign evaluation
   (f) Market
   (g) Product
   (h) Other

8. Overseas operations ☐ (5)

9. Personal relationships and professional capability of: ☐ (15)
   (a) Account executive
   (b) Account director
   (c) Chairman
   (d) Managing director

10. Meeting scheduled dates ☐ (5)

CHOOSING A
CONSULTANCY

For every organization, there is somewhere a public relations consultancy which will do an extremely good job for them—the problem is finding it. The following gives a three-stage operation comprising coarse screening, fine screening and, finally, the pitch. Examples are given from the UK, though the process has equal validity anywhere in the world, except the reference sources will be different.

Coarse screening

The starting point is to draw up a consultancy specification outlining all the services required together with the nature of the organization, such as its size, location, number of clients (largest and smallest), fee structure, staff specializations, and so on.

What is required now is a list of 12 candidate consultancies. These will be found by reference to a directory (e.g. *Hollis Press and Public Relations Annual* and *Public Relations Consultants Association Yearbook*) listing all the consultancies in a given country together with their clients, and maybe other useful information. You are not looking for a consultancy handling a competitive account because this would not be acceptable by the trade association nor the competitor and, anyway, would be undesirable. Many consultancies actually have associate companies for just this situation. Rather, you are looking for a firm thoroughly well acquainted with the same markets and publics, known to have very effective public relations, but non-competitive.

Address a letter to the CEO of each consultancy, in confidence, asking whether or not they would feel able to handle such a new client and, if so, to write giving such details as they thought appropriate. The letter would, of course, be accompanied by the specification. Replies will mostly be prompt and enthusiastic, but they will vary greatly to such an extent as to make the selection of the best three quite an easy task.

At the coarse screening stage, you will obviously consult with colleagues and contacts as well as any existing file of propositions sent in cold over the past year or so. A major source of guidance here is to make contact with two or three friendly journalists to ask for recommendations. Such is the relationship between journalists and public relations consultancies, if a journalist makes a recommendation, there is a fair chance it will turn out to be a good one.

Fine screening

Send a letter to the three shortlisted candidates indicating your wish to proceed further. This will result in a visit to the consultancy for what is referred to as a *credentials presentation* when they will present examples of relevant campaigns. It is as well to remember these are the best (so what are the worst like?). This stage can even be regarded as more important than the pitch which might follow since, in each case, it is hoped there was enough time and experience to do a thorough job, whereas many pitches are hastily prepared and, as a result, too superficial and not always indicative of the best work the consultancy is capable of producing. A useful follow-up to this presentation is to make personal contact with all of the clients involved to get a view from the other side. A further follow-up is to have each of the consultancies pay you a visit, just to see how they would relate to you and your colleagues on 'home ground'.

The pitch

Hopefully, all three candidates will survive the fine screening and will now be prepared to move on to the final stage. Here, each one should be given a carefully prepared written brief outlining what would be required of them should they win the account. They must have the opportunity of asking for elaboration on any point they choose, and obviously must have a reasonable time in which to prepare, in effect, an outline communications plan. Should the client pay a fee? There is no easy answer to this. Most times there is no fee, even though the trade association may recommend there should be.

Regarding the final presentation, it is as well to make sure the presentation team is actually the one which is going to work on the account or the whole operation is a waste of time. No doubt there will be a small group of client executives with an appropriate checklist for performance comparisons. The core of the checklist will be the initial specification. The final, and most important, question should be 'Would I enjoy working with this person?' If the answer is 'Yes', then hire them. If 'No', then forget it. There are already far too many client companies who just do not get on well with their consultancy, and where a future breakup is inevitable. It is preferable to repeat the whole process rather than harness up with a consultancy which will prove to be inadequate, incompetent, or otherwise unacceptable.

One final observation. Early on a would-be consultancy is going to ask, 'What is the budget?' The answer here is simply you had hoped they would advise you on the budget once they had received the briefing. After all, this is the single most important matter to be decided. What you want to learn from an independent and professional source is just what expenditure is necessary, as opposed to what you have spent in the past or what you can afford. Obviously, you can give some indication of the order of investment you would anticipate but, after all, you might be quite wrong—in either direction.

ASSESSING STAFF SKILLS AND COMPETENCIES

Where do public relations practitioners come from? There used to be a simple answer to this question: from journalism. But today a public relations executive must have an all-round capability in every form of communication. A background in marketing communications is likely to be most useful.

The next question has to be whether or not public relations can be learned by education or training, or can it come only from experience? For many years a strong school of thought has claimed public relations cannot be taught. Such a proposition has been shown to be untrue in the US, and the same is now being demonstrated all over the world. There are many elements of public relations practice which can, and have to be, taught: research into target audiences, for instance, planning and budgeting, inter- and intra-media comparisons, typography, and so on.

While academic courses and qualifications are extremely important, and their number is growing, a major activity is in the field of training. The following outline and tables come from the 'Public Relations Education and Training Matrix'*, produced in the UK jointly by the Institute of Public Relations and the Public Relations Consultants Association.

The matrix has been designed as a basis for:

• self-assessment of training needs and career development

• appraisal of employees' skills and their development needs

• evaluation of training and education course suitability.

It is in four categories:

• Knowledge

• Business skills

• Public relations skills—counsel and planning

• Public relations skills—implementation

---

* *Produced with the kind permission of the Institute of Public Relations and the Public Relations Consultants Association*

Five stages of knowledge skills or experience have been identified:

Stage 1: **Pre-entry requirements**—basic skills and knowledge necessary for any candidate wishing to pursue a career in public relations; these may be developed while working in an administrative role.

Stage 2: **Professional starter**—specific knowledge and skills essential for those developing their public relations career, from assistants and junior executives

Stages: **Developing and operating professional**—development, knowledge and skills, 3 & 4: necessarily gained over a period of time, to become a fully rounded and experienced public relations practitioner

Stage 5: **Experienced professional specialist and manager**—the continuing development phase from functional to team or group supervision responsibility, senior counselling and management

KNOWLEDGE	STAGE 1	2	3	4	5
1. The role of public relations, both in-house and consultancy, in commercial and public sector organization	✓	✓	✓	✓	✓
2 An appreciation of the range of techniques and media available to public relations practitioners	✓	✓	✓	✓	✓
3 The role, responsibilities, vocabulary, techniques, ethics, law and regulations relating to: – public relations	✓	✓	✓	✓	✓
– marketing, advertising, research and behavioral studies, sales promotion, direct marketing, direct selling		✓	✓	✓	✓
4 The role, responsibilities, vocabulary, techniques, ethics, law and regulations relating to: – print and broadcast media, publishing, telecommunications		✓	✓	✓	✓
– sponsorship		✓	✓	✓	✓
5 The structure, priorities, distribution, basic economics, organization and operation of: – manufacturing industry		✓	✓	✓	✓
– service industries		✓	✓	✓	✓
– financial institutions		✓	✓	✓	✓
– central and local government		✓	✓	✓	✓
– the public sector		✓	✓	✓	✓
– voluntary organizations		✓	✓	✓	✓
– membership bodies		✓	✓	✓	✓
– the professions		✓	✓	✓	✓
6 The legal, legislative and regulatory framework				✓	✓
7 Organizational strategy and policy making, both concept and practice			✓	✓	✓
8 Managerial psychological/organizational hierarchy – communication				✓	✓
– motivation				✓	✓
– leadership/team building				✓	✓

	BUSINESS SKILLS		STAGE 1	2	3	4	5
1	Communications:	Telephone technique	✓	✓	✓	✓	✓
2		Meeting technique	✓	✓	✓	✓	✓
3		Presentation technique		✓	✓	✓	✓
4		Working as part of a team	✓	✓	✓	✓	✓
5		Working as part of an organization		✓	✓	✓	✓
6		Networking (clients, colleagues, contacts)		✓	✓	✓	✓
7		Induction and orientation				✓	✓
8	Organizational:	Workflow planning and setting priorities	✓	✓	✓	✓	✓
9		Interviewing and staff selection				✓	✓
10		Time management		✓	✓	✓	✓
11		Delegation and supervision		✓	✓	✓	✓
12		Motivation and leadership			✓	✓	✓
13		Budget setting and control			✓	✓	✓
14		Team building and management				✓	✓
15		Training and development of individuals and teams				✓	✓
16		Understanding and design of financial controls				✓	✓
17		Understanding/design of quality controls, including ISO 9000				✓	✓
18	Analytical:	Analyzing annual reports and financial data			✓	✓	✓
19		Understanding the use of research data			✓	✓	✓
20		Desk research		✓	✓	✓	✓
21		Communication audits			✓	✓	✓

	PUBLIC RELATIONS SKILLS – COUNSEL AND PLANNING	STAGE				
		1	2	3	4	5
1	Understanding public relations objectives and strategies		✓	✓	✓	✓
2	Identifying publics		✓	✓	✓	✓
3	Understanding the differing emphasis of various market sectors, such as: – consumer, technical, financial, health and science			✓	✓	✓
4	Formulating public relations objectives			✓	✓	✓
5	Developing public relations strategies, both overall and contingency			✓	✓	✓
6	Creating public relations plans for action			✓	✓	✓
7	Monitoring and evaluating progress and delivery			✓	✓	✓
8	Assessing public relations implications of general management plans and decisions				✓	✓
9	Identifying trends, risks and issues relevant to an organization			✓	✓	✓
10	Assessing the public relations implications for an organization of the plans and decisions of other organizations, including: – its market place – local and national government – the European Union – national and international regulatory bodies – the media – special interest groups – the local community			✓ ✓ ✓ ✓ ✓ ✓ ✓	✓ ✓ ✓ ✓ ✓ ✓ ✓	✓ ✓ ✓ ✓ ✓ ✓ ✓
11	Understanding the implications of international developments in the media			✓	✓	✓
12	Counselling and advisory techniques				✓	✓
13	Risk analysis and issue management				✓	✓
14	Crisis management				✓	✓

PUBLIC RELATIONS SKILLS – IMPLEMENTATION	STAGE				
	1	2	3	4	5
1 Business writing:					
– agendas, meeting notes, memoranda, letters	✓	✓	✓	✓	✓
– reports, proposals, planning, progress		✓	✓	✓	✓
2 Editorial writing:					
– photocalls, media alerts, photo captions, draft releases	✓	✓	✓	✓	✓
– briefing and feature material, newsletters, proofreading		✓	✓	✓	✓
– script development and writing			✓	✓	✓
3 Speeches and presentations			✓	✓	✓
4 Selecting media to reach identified publics		✓	✓	✓	✓
5 Compiling contact lists	✓	✓	✓	✓	✓
6 Media liaison techniques and operation			✓	✓	✓
7 Editorial planning and monitoring			✓	✓	✓
8 Editorial promotions (competitions, reader offers)			✓	✓	✓
9 Negotiating editorial features and interviews			✓	✓	✓
10 Handling editorial inquiries		✓	✓	✓	✓
11 Selecting external resources: photographer, designers, printers and researchers			✓	✓	✓
12 The basics of photography		✓	✓	✓	✓
13 Briefing a photographer			✓	✓	✓
14 Event planning and management			✓	✓	✓
15 Exhibition planning and management			✓	✓	✓
16 Sponsorship selection, planning and organization			✓	✓	✓
17 Briefing designers			✓	✓	✓
18 Print selection, briefing and production management			✓	✓	✓
19 Capabilities of desktop publishing			✓	✓	✓
20 Audio/visual briefing and production management			✓	✓	✓
21 VNR/B-Roll production and distribution			✓	✓	✓
22 Radio production and placement		✓	✓	✓	
23 Public speaking				✓	✓
24 Giving interviews				✓	✓
25 Conference and seminar participation				✓	✓

PUBLIC RELATIONS
PUBLICS AUDIT

These are the many discrete and homogeneous groups of people whose opinion is of importance to an organization. Sometimes referred to as stakeholders, they are the target audiences for any public relations campaign and will be an intrinsic component of it.

Marketing publics

These comprise the entire customer base together with prospective and past customers. It is necessary to go further and identify all the people who go to make up the decision-making unit (DMU), since most purchasing decisions are made by, or influenced by, more than one person. In consumer marketing, various members of a family might be involved; for instance, a child might eat a breakfast cereal, a mother purchase it, a father pay for it, and then various relatives and friends express points of view.

In business to business marketing, the DMU is rather more complicated. In the first place, someone is going to specify a product or service is required. This, in turn, may be influenced by any number of people within the organization, even though they may have no actual authority. Next comes the group which does have authority and, for a major purchase, is likely to involve the entire board of directors. Then the transaction has to be undertaken by a purchasing department involving one or more executives.

Another possibility to be allowed for is what is termed a 'gatekeeper'. This is anyone in a position to intercept a selling message, e.g. a secretary blocking a direct mailshot, a telephone call, or a visit; similarly with a receptionist and a telephonist.

The final category is the user. This might be just one person, but it might be hundreds. The whole point is, when referring to a customer or prospect, one is not usually dealing with just one individual but with many. In an industrial purchasing transaction there could, typically, be 10 people involved, each with their own sectional interests affecting the messages to be sent, and each with their own quite separate media.

The very real concept of the DMU does not apply just to the marketing area. With other public relations publics there are many individuals to be influenced behind one single targeted audience. A local authority, for instance, is not just one unit, but rather a whole range of elected representatives together with permanent officials. In marketing, the following six categories should be allowed for:

• specifier

• influencer

• authorizer

• buyer

• gatekeeper

• user.

In considering marketing publics, special note should be taken of competitors and whether any special campaign is required here. The same might be said of suppliers, though this is more the concern of the purchasing department or production.

A final category in the marketing arena, and sometimes a critical one, is what might be termed *third-party audiences*. The principal one here, of course, is the retailer and this must take in, where appropriate, all the shop assistants and other retail staff. Their good opinion of one organization against another can be the deciding factor in the purchasing process; for example, 'You can rely on this firm', or 'Their backup service is excellent'. Then there are business partners, agents, distributors, and trade associations.

Personnel or human resource (HR) publics

The first group of people to consider here are employees, not forgetting the growing number of hired-in staff. Also include employees' families, past employees, future employees, and any employee organizations, such as trade unions. It is not good enough just to say all employees; the individual groupings must be identified since their current performance in terms of perceptions and behavior may well be different, and the media must also be selected to be the most suitable. An internal attitude audit would use a checklist rather like the following:

• CEO

• directors

• management

• salespeople

• service staff

• reception

• telephonists

• secretaries

• drivers

• operatives

• security

• canteen

• cleaners.

Also under the human resources umbrella will be the local community and local government. To be seen as a good neighbor with a local social responsibility, caring for people and the environment, can be an important factor in recruitment and in any development projects. The general public in the locality needs to be supplemented by special attention given to local opinion formers and, indeed, local decision makers and include such groupings as doctors, police, solicitors, teachers, club leaders, the clergy, councillors, local authority staff, plus, of course, all local media.

Financial publics

The start here is with shareholders, to which must be added potential shareholders and past shareholders. Do any of these groups have DMUs? Institutional shareholders do, for example. But what about the influencers? Here the list is long and is often subsumed by a title other than financial public relations, namely *investor relations* (IR). The publics to be included here are stockbrokers, financial analysts, banks, accountancy practices, and any other intermediaries. The financial media obviously play an important part.

Corporate publics

These are groups of people whose opinions are expected to affect the business as a whole rather than just one part of it alone, e.g. customers. A major part of this operation is in dealing with national government relations and lobbying. Here, one must make provision for all the elected representatives and prospective candidates, together with civil servants in the ministries who might have some impact on a particular organization's interests. Action on a national basis must then be extended, where appropriate, to regional bodies such as the European Union, and then on to international bodies. Provision must also be made somewhere for international public relations, which may come solely under the marketing umbrella but may extend into other functions where there are overseas plants as well as agents.

There will be other groups which need to be handled at a corporate level, and these will vary according to the organization's particular interests. Employers' professional and trade associations would fall into this category, as would many special-interest groups and opinion formers.

SELECTING THE MEDIA

All media channels have their limitations and thus, in order to communicate effectively, it is usually necessary to employ a combination referred to as the 'media mix'.

Media strengths and weaknesses

Editorial publicity. Whether news stories or feature articles, these are far more credible than advertisements in the same publications since they have the implied endorsement of the publication. Furthermore, there are up to five times the number of readers and, after all, it is free. As against this, there is no control over whether or not the story will ever appear, and if does, whether it will be complimentary or even accurate. And it will certainly not appear more than once. The opportunity to have reprints is a bonus. Major national or international news stories may well cause a blackout on other news. Even so, it is the most cost-effective medium.

Press advertising. Strengths and weaknesses here are the opposite to those of editorial publicity. The strengths are an ad is fully controllable as to when and where it appears, what it says, how large it is, and when it should be repeated. The weaknesses are it is expensive, has fewer readers, and is obviously biased. It is also probably the least cost-effective channel.

Exhibitions. It is not generally realized just how cost effective an exhibition can be. Its particular claim to fame lies in its productivity so far as personal one-to-one interviews are concerned. A staff person will meet with as many visitors in an hour on an exhibition stand than he or she would do in a day on the road. Furthermore, with an exhibition the buyer is calling on the seller, in effect saying, 'May I have information about your product or company'; the opposite of the normal selling situation and obviously a psychological plus. Go on from this benefit to the unique opportunity to demonstrate a products, get personal feedback on its operation and application, not to mention the corporate image value, and the exhibition will be seen to have been undervalued. The downside is high basic cost and the internal disruption for weeks before and after the exhibition. Also, of course, the number and quality of visitors might be disappointing, and include what are referred to as 'tire kickers', i.e. waste time and seem mainly concerned with collecting leaflets.

Direct mail. This must be communication's shooting star. The strengths are obviously messages can be sent directly to the target audience which will at least see them before disposing of them. Furthermore, the creative opportunities are many. Any material can be used—plastic, metal, glass, as well as paper and cardboard. It can appeal to a number of senses—sight, hearing, touch, even smell. Samples can be sent, large catalogs, audio and videotapes, and so on. Direct mail is renowned for its response capability. Its most significant limitation is inaccuracy of databases which, in any case, age by around 20 percent per annum. The problem is sometimes also defining with accuracy the members of the 'decision-making units'. And unless a person can be identified, he or she cannot be written to. There is also an increasing problem of imagery, i.e. rubbish mailing, and this will probably get worse.

Television advertising. This is overwhelmingly the medium of high-impact mass communication with the opportunity of mixing movement with sound and color, and doing it fast. For highly segmented markets, the wastage can be vast and the cost astronomical, including production. Direct response here is also difficult. It is regarded by many as intrusive.

Radio advertising. Segmentation is easier than for television, and is of great value for local community campaigns. Radio costs less than television, but the impact is less as well.

Cinema. This is essentially a medium with a very precise focus on two age groups, i.e. teens and forties. It is not usually suitable for a public relations campaign.

Posters. A very precise medium for consumer marketing, providing the message is simple, posters are of little application in public relations other than in very special circumstances, such as exhibition halls, airports and railway stations.

Telemarketing. Another growth area, this is increasingly used as a follow-up system on direct mail campaigns where the two together go under the label of direct marketing. Its strength is in making personal contact with speed and impact, fixing appointments and, increasingly, gaining data and responses to support marketing research programs.

The media mix

For effective communication, it is not often possible to rely on just one or two media; rather more likely is the need to select by methodical analysis an optimum combination of media categories to achieve the desired effect. A media mix is required to make a thorough and positive communication with all the publics involved with a particular organization.

Inter-media comparisons

To arrive at an effective media mix data must be available on which to make comparative judgments. In consumer advertising there is a relatively wide range of research material available to assist the media planner but, even here, the task is extraordinarily difficult. In the industrial sector one is hard pressed to obtain even the most elementary information. As a result, if guesswork is to be avoided, at least some form of logical grid must be devised against which each possible medium must be evaluated and given a certain comparative rating. Figure 6 is an example of a typical grid.

The list of promotional media shown in Figure 6 is by no means exhaustive and would differ from one company to another. In just the same way, the criteria for media choice may vary depending, for instance, on whether the target market is a consumer or industrial one. The following 12 factors and the use of a matrix are regarded as no more than an aid to planning for a public relations campaign.

FIGURE 6
INTER-MEDIA GRID

	Market size	Intrinsic impact	Message	Coverage & penetration	Negative characteristics	Positive characteristics	Cost	Speed	Complexity & convenience	Feedback	Creative scope	Data availability
Newspapers												
Magazines												
Television												
Radio												
Cinema												
Posters												
Point of purchase												
Telephone												
Exhibitions												
Editorials												
Sponsorship												
Direct mail												
Directories												

**FIGURE 7
AUDIENCE SIZE GRID**

	100	1,00	10,000	100,000	1,000,000
Personal Contact					
Letters/DM					
Telephone					
Demonstration					
Seminars					
Conference					
Private Exhibition					
Public Exhibition					
Literature					
AV					
Editorial Publicity					
Press Advertising					
Radio Advertising					
TV Advertising					
Poster Advertising					
Sponsorship					

1. *Audience.* The total size of a target audience or market segment and all of the people comprising it must be the starting point of media choice. With 10 units, there is clearly not much room for more than personal contact supported by whatever backup might be required. Move to 100 units and the situation hardly changes. At 1000 the personal contact must become selective, and here one can add direct mail, specialized press advertising, editorial publicity, literature, perhaps sponsored films and AV, local demonstrations and maybe telephone calls. At 10,000, personal contact falls away and press advertising and other non-personal media take over. Public exhibitions have particular merit, combining unit economy with the benefits of face-to-face contact. Direct mail sometimes starts to become difficult to handle. Editorial backup is, of course, worth full exploitation. At

42

100,000, one starts to move into mass media, with television, radio, national newspapers and posters replacing or heavily supplementing the other media already listed. Figure 7 indicates how media choice varies with audience size.

2. *Impact.* The extent to which a promotional message is transmitted, received, stored, and is able to be recalled with accuracy is vital. Each medium has its own intrinsic impact potential. Clearly a medium which facilitates two-way communication is top of the list, and so personal contact, exhibitions, demonstrations, and telephone calls are all worthy of a high rating. Direct mail, properly conceived, can expect to perform well here, as can editorial publicity, sponsored films and literature. All the research evidence on page traffic and Starch (US) measurements indicates press advertising performs least well in achieving impact. Television, on the other hand, has a high, if transitory, impact potential.

3. *Message.* What is the nature of the message? Is it simple, or a reminder? Is it complex, technical or innovative? In the former case television, press advertising, point of purchase, posters and radio will do well. For a complicated message, however, the need is for demonstrations, seminars, feature articles, literature, sponsored films and personal contact.

4. *Coverage and penetration.* This is the breadth and depth of a medium's capability. In breadth, the question is what proportion of the target audience is covered by readership as opposed to circulation. In other words, will they have an 'opportunity to see'? In direct mail the answer could be 100 percent, with a national newspaper perhaps 40 percent. Commonly, you are looking for in-depth coverage of around 80 percent. Turning to penetration, certain media are known by long-standing practice to penetrate decision-making units even where the people involved cannot be identified: a major trade fair, for instance, or a weekly trade magazine seen by anyone who wants to keep up to date.

5. *Negative characteristics.* Some people resent some advertising and it is as well to check out in advance of using a particular media group whether this could be, in any way, counterproductive. Most people in the UK, for instance, dislike advertising messages on the telephone, or salespeople at the front door or on the street corner. They also dislike loose inserts, direct mail which is too expensive or repetitive, and radio and television commercials are often seen to be intrusive. It depends on many factors—just check it out.

6. *Positive characteristics.* Is there an added plus which comes over and above the basic medium itself? Examples include an ad in a very prestigious publication where to be seen in good company lends an extra credibility to an advertising proposition. With an exhibition stand, a comfortable lounge can be a welcome oasis after the formal business has been completed. An in-house exhibition or

seminar might draw together people with common interests who have not met for some time and who welcome the chance of informal discussion almost as much as the event itself.

7. *Cost.* There are two costs to be considered as well as price. The first cost is the total capital investment involved and whether this is compatible with the cashflow position, and also the other major expenditures on communication activities. Then the cost per contact must be evaluated. Media planning decisions are often made on the outcome of aggressive media buying, and this is where price comes in. All rate cards have their price—10 percent off quoted rates can be a lot of money, and is a worthwhile objective.

8. *Speed.* Television, radio, newspapers, direct mail, all under pressure can be transmitting messages within 24 hours or less, and to very large audiences simultaneously. At the other extreme, it might be two years before an appropriate trade fair takes place. Thus, if the time for activating consumer/customer behavior is a critical factor, then choice of media must be influenced by this.

9. *Complexity and convenience.* Nothing could be simpler than to take $1 million and allocate it to a single commercial network on television, and the balance to full pages in national newspapers. Such a media strategy may even be right. Compare this to the complexity of a multimarket, multishot direct mail campaign, coupled with regional presentations tied in with local public relations, regional press, supporting literature and posters, with a culminating business gift. Media choice might be influenced by ease of use (idleness), coupled with other non-professional factors such as good or bad agency commission. Media choice must therefore have some regard to the amount of effort required to service each medium (a cost) in relation to the income and aggravation it is likely to receive.

10. *Feedback.* Examine any advertising medium and you will find the great majority of advertisements invite no explicit response in the way of direct feedback, and thus they receive very little. Hence press advertising and television are essentially single-channel communication systems. Since impact is greater where a dialog can be established, there must be an intrinsic advantage in all the face-to-face media, and even with direct mail and editorial publicity there are some instances of feedback. Many of the popular sales promotion techniques actively invite the customer's participation.

11. *Creative scope.* Should a medium be chosen for its creative scope? Increasingly this is regarded as a major factor but within the rather strict limits of availability of color or movement. What is meant here is the opportunity for some quite novel or extraordinary approach to be made entirely as a result of the medium being used. In press relations, the creative opportunities to set up an extremely newsworthy event are limitless and, needless to say, this would be done in such a way as to

involve the product or company inextricably. With direct mail there is complete freedom on material, size, shape, color, smell, timing, audience and frequency. Exhibitions also have an almost infinite variety of creative opportunities. Particularly where the message itself is mundane, the choice of media for creativity is especially relevant.

12. *Data availability*. There is a somewhat old-fashioned idea in public relations that, since the amounts of money to be spent are relatively small, the need for information about what one is buying is not very great. This is a quite extraordinary and illogical situation since the task may well be of the greatest importance to the company; the cost of achieving not being astronomical does not mean the media buying operation should be incompetent.

With any media overlapping into consumer marketing, a good deal of information is likely to be available, but otherwise it is hard to find. The technical press is rarely able to provide believable readership data. Some advertisers set up their own sources of audience information and possibly, in respect of 'data', media choice should be biased towards those channels from which the most reliable facts can be obtained.

Other choices in media

Over and above the mainstream media, many other activities and channels are worthy of consideration. These include those shown in Table 3 overleaf.

TABLE 3

External media

- Private exhibitions
- Seminars and conferences
- Audio/video
- Presentations
- Road shows
- Works visits
- Disks
- House magazines (internal, external, audio)
- Customer user panels
- Dealer panels
- Letters
- Gifts
- Helplines
- Competitions
- Social events
- Corporate hospitality
- Books
- Newsletters
- Complaints
- Mailing: ads and press releases
- Training
- Literature
- Case studies

Internal media

- Noticeboards
- Pay packet inserts
- Special launch brochures
- Training sessions
- Trade union representatives
- Campaign presentations
- Static displays
- Special competitions
- Congratulations boards
- VIP visits
- Award ceremonies
- Company magazines
- Manager/employee team talks
- Senior management presentations
- Mass meetings
- Specialist consultants
- Videos/audiocassettes
- Posters
- Information on personal computers
- Attitude surveys
- Local newspaper articles
- Sports and social activities
- Literature
- Annual reports

GOOD MEDIA RELATIONS

In any public relations marketing communications campaigns, the value of good editorial publicity is as great as any other message source, if not greater. Furthermore, it is probably the most cost-effective channel of communication, and thus should be exploited to the full. In broad terms, editorial publicity falls into three categories—news, features and comment.

Journalists are overwhelmed with information from all types of organizations wanting free and supportive publicity. Whether they get it, and whether it is both correct and positive, depends in large measure on the goodwill of a whole host of journalists and the extent to which they are well informed and motivated.

An essential exercise is to compile a list of media whose support might be said to be critical to an organization's success. This represents an active and ongoing program of action in making the acquaintance of the key journalists and in maintaining the relationship. The occasional working lunch is probably the best possible way of structuring such a program. From among the hoards of incoming press releases, yours will, as a consequence, stand out from the others as maybe worth a second glance. Furthermore, when, say, an industry issue arises on which a journalist wants an outside comment, this will more than likely come from someone with whom the journalist has a personal contact. Since a substantial amount of media coverage comes out of press releases, or more properly 'news releases', it may be useful to look at the basic ground rules.

Guidelines on news releases

The guiding principle is 'If in doubt, leave it out', but generally a story should run to between 100 and 300 words. It should be written in the same style as a journalist would write it, i.e. giving the news as it will interest the reader. And it should be written in a factual, authoritative manner; it should be lively and interesting, but without the smallest trace of the hard sell.

A good rule to follow is to adopt an inverted triangle with the really important news at the top and the supporting information coming further down. This enables a news editor to sub from the bottom and still leave intact the main thrust of the story.

Structure. As with any piece of writing, it must have a beginning, a middle, and an end.

Headline. This is vital. It must make the journalist pause and read on, rather than put the release into the bin. So write the essential news in three or four words. And play it straight. No journalist will use your headline. If they did, they might find a competitive publication doing the same thing, so they just will not take the risk.

First paragraph. The release stands or falls on the first paragraph. It must contain the main news angle written from the reader's point of view, not from yours. The basic marketing concept is identify the consumer benefit.

Second and third paragraphs. If these are necessary, they are there to elaborate on the main story already told in the first paragraph. But even so, they must only give the highlights of what you are trying to put across. It is not nearly so interesting to the reader as it is to you.

Fourth paragraph. Consider putting in a quote from someone in authority, preferably outside the organization and therefore more credible.

Fifth paragraph. Include facts and data here such as price, delivery, the date an event will happen, and so on.

Further information. Always offer this: give two names to contact, with office and home telephone and fax numbers.

Points to note:

1. Keep sentences short; avoid jargon and abbreviations.

2. Have a clear, attractive layout, typed on one side only, double-spaced with wide margins.

3. Send the release only to media which will really find it of interest.

4. Use a photograph wherever possible, and always caption it so the caption can be seen at the same time as the photograph.

5. Any amplification of the story should be on separate sheets or in an accompanying publication which can be used or discarded, depending on its relevance to the journalist. Use a different color paper to the release itself.

6. Ask journalists to criticize your releases. That's the way to learn.

7. At the bottom of page one, if it continues, write 'more follows', and at the end, 'Ends'.

8. Always put the date of the release and an embargo if there is one, but only the latter if absolutely necessary.

9. Include contact name or names with telephone and fax numbers for all times of the day or night.

10. Paragraphs should be short—40 words or so.

11. Avoid superlatives and exaggerated claims. Always write in the style of the publication, as if the editor or journalist had written it.

What makes news?

This will vary from organization to organization, but Table 4 is a checklist of 20 items to which can be added any specialized topics.

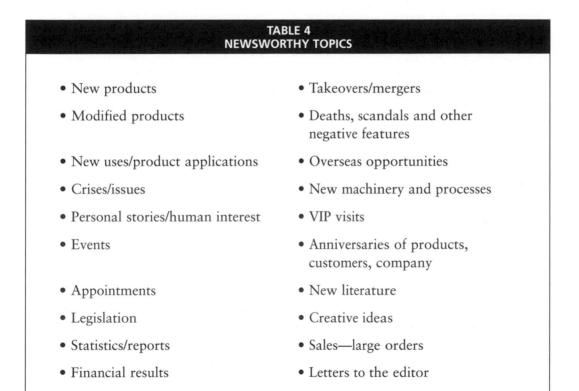

TABLE 4 NEWSWORTHY TOPICS	
• New products	• Takeovers/mergers
• Modified products	• Deaths, scandals and other negative features
• New uses/product applications	• Overseas opportunities
• Crises/issues	• New machinery and processes
• Personal stories/human interest	• VIP visits
• Events	• Anniversaries of products, customers, company
• Appointments	• New literature
• Legislation	• Creative ideas
• Statistics/reports	• Sales—large orders
• Financial results	• Letters to the editor

For radio stations and television networks, there is an increasing and successful use of video news releases and their equivalent audiotapes.

In some parts of the world, the publishing of editorial material, whether features, news or comment, depends on the placing of some supporting advertising. It is as well to find out what might be regarded as the norm, and then conform to it. This happens mostly with lesser publications and is obviously something to be discouraged and overcome, if possible. After all, the quality of a publication cannot be great if the criterion for editorial inclusion is the size of the advertising budget, as against the intrinsic news value.

In support of, and sometimes in addition to, news releases there are press receptions and press visits, both of which have a valid part to play in any media relations activity.

Press receptions

As a generalization, there are too many of these and the press do not like them. They do have a value but it must be for an item of news really important to the media concerned, and where there is a need for questions to be asked and answered, and/or for a demonstration, or for a number of one-to-one interviews. Journalists are not going to ask key questions in an open forum. They do not need an exotic and expensive venue to attract them to come, merely some news, event or information of value.

Press visits

By and large, journalists like press visits. It may involve half a day or even more, but they welcome the opportunity of getting out and about in industry and commerce and meeting people of influence behind the scenes. It is important for such an event to be well done, and journalists expect to be well looked after. Good hospitality coupled with a good number of well-informed and well-motivated staff is a prerequisite. Not only can one expect to get good, well-informed coverage, but the visit also helps to cement relationships further for other times and events.

PUBLIC RELATIONS EVALUATION

Evaluation must start with the strategic objectives of corporate image. These should not be difficult to measure and track, providing they have been quantified in the first instance. From there, a great amount of detail can be examined to ensure each of the component parts is performing well. These will include a number of criteria for editorial publicity together with all the other media channels to be employed, such as advertising, exhibitions, direct mail etc. Table 5 is a checklist of typical communications channels together with some criteria for their evaluation. Part of the work necessary can easily be carried out in-house, such as monitoring press cuttings. Others might require the use of an outside research facility. No doubt time and money will be required to support such an operation, but it is vital it be done. How else can one know the public relations investment is achieving the goals set?

TABLE 5
EVALUATING COMMUNICATIONS CHANNELS

Corporate image:

- Awareness

- Attitude

- Behavioral intent

- Behavior

Editorial publicity:

- Number of publications (database)/releases (distribution)

- Number of press cuttings—conversion rate

- Column inches (cms)—quantitative and qualitative (positive/negative) – accurate/inaccurate

- OTS (opportunity to see)

- Advertisement equivalent

- Inquiries/bingo cards

- Analysis—monthly, cumulative

TABLE 5 *continued*

Other publicity

- Events—participants and editorials

- Competitions—competitors

- Road shows—visitors

- Advertisements—recall and inquiries

- Direct mail—responses

- Exhibitions—visitors/inquiries/leaflets

- Seminars—delegates

- Videos—showings/audience

THE TEN-POINT PUBLIC RELATIONS
ACTION PLAN

A public relations plan can be broken down into 10 discrete steps. Some might argue the opening stage should be research rather than objectives, a fair point. If all the necessary information for compiling the plan is not available, it is clearly necessary to conduct research into the various publics concerned and, indeed, into any other matter required. If this has been done, work should proceed as follows.

Step One—Objectives

These should comprise a clear statement of the aims of the plan, having regard to the business objectives. They should be simple to understand, unambiguous and, most importantly, quantified. So many plans in the past have set out to achieve 'an increase in awareness' of a given organization. What must be asked is by how much, by whom, and by when. There is clearly no way in which a campaign can be evaluated unless there is a tangible, and thus measurable, objective. Furthermore, how can a budget possibly be set without knowing precisely what the benefit is going to be. With objectives centered around perceptions, it is necessary to refine further what these should be, i.e. produce a list of qualities or attributes with which the organization desires to be associated. The sum total of these might be said to make up what is, in effect, a corporate personality. This takes the current attributes, compares them with those it wishes to be perceived, and then draws up a program designed to close any gaps. There is every reason for such attributes to be scaled so performance is quantified and thus measurable. These would include integrity, value for money, technical innovation, social responsibility, service, reliability, imagination, confidence, etc.

Step Two—Issues

The question here is: 'Are there any issues, internal or external, which would undermine the achievement of the objectives?' The state of the economy might be an important factor, as might unhelpful staff attitudes. If the communications objective is to establish a firm as the technological leader in the field, this will be of no avail if part of the product range has poor performance. Indeed, it may be necessary to change the objectives in view of the existence of certain issues.

Step Three—Strategy

There should be no confusion between objectives, strategy and plan. Quite simply, the objective is what we aim to achieve, the strategy is how we aim to achieve it, and the plan is the details of the program of activities to take place. The strategy sets down in brief the policy for reaching the objective, i.e. 'by means of'.

Step Four—Audiences (External and Internal)

In order to achieve the greatest cost-effectiveness for a public relations campaign, there are two essentials. First there is a need to fine tune each of the publics into narrow groups with the same homogeneous characteristics, and in industrial or business markets this means identifying the people belonging to the decision-making unit, not just the organizations. The second, and equally important, ingredient is to quantify the people concerned. In addition to external audiences, the internal market should be included, i.e. employees, as well as intermediaries, such as business partners.

Step Five—Messages

These should not be a statement of the *attributes* of an organization. Rather, it is a matter of identifying the benefits. After all, engineers can be said not to buy drills but rather to buy holes. One can even argue customers only buy 'perceived benefits', and so if a customer thinks he or she is getting satisfaction, to all intents and purposes he or she is. Thus, messages must be transmitted to satisfy the 'needs' or 'wants' of a prospect, which more usefully might be termed 'requirements'. And messages need to be prioritized and tailored to fit each person in the DMU.

Step Six—Media Plan

These are the channels of communication through which the messages are to be sent to the target audiences. The plan shows how each of the component parts relates to the others in both time, messages, and what might be termed corporate identity. They will be matched to each of the target audiences for minimum wastage. Media might include advertising, editorial publicity, exhibitions, direct mail, seminars, road shows, etc. Remember also the media for the internal market.

Step Seven—Timetable

This usually spans a year, possibly on a rolling basis. A shorter timescale might be employed, and it is certainly useful to give some indication of a longer period ahead. In practice, one can see how a direct mail campaign will support an exhibition, and how a press release is timed to avoid being scooped by an advertisement carrying the same story. It is recommended to use a Gantt chart, and to make provision for periodic reviews.

Step Eight—Budget

The planning stage is the earliest time at which it is possible to produce a budget. There is no sensible reason for starting out with a sum of money, and figuring out how best to spend it. It may be far too much or far too little. But by working progressively and logically through each of the steps, having regard to the task to be achieved, the production of a budget is simply a matter of costing all the various items built into the plan.

Step Nine—Measurement

Campaign evaluation is both vital and simple, providing the objectives are clear and quantified. Furthermore, it is important to carry out some form of tracking in order to make adjustments to the campaign if targets are not being met. The only relevant criteria are the communications objectives, as opposed, for instance, marketing objectives. Thus, to measure 'sales' is quite unacceptable since they will have been influenced by other factors such as product performance, price, delivery, and, indeed, the efficacy of the salesforce. Typical communications objectives are awareness and perception.

Step Ten—Resources

This relates to human resources, both in terms of the number of people to be involved in implementing the campaign, and in their professional capability to carry out the work involved with maximum efficiency. This part of the plan should also take in the use of outside services such as the public relations consultancy. Here also is where any training needs and expense should be covered.

Notes

Introduction. Included in any background notes should be such internal and external factors as PEEST (political, economic, environmental, sociological, technological) and SWOT (strengths, weaknesses, opportunities, threats).

Research. Should any essential factors be unknown, provision should be made for initial research over and above what will be conducted at the 'evaluation' stage.

Quantifying. Particular attention should be paid to quantifying objectives and target audiences as well as a media breakdown.

Media plan. This should represent the main body of the report and list the media in detail, but also the rationale for using those chosen and those rejected.

Budgets. Budgets should be task oriented, bottom up rather than top down, using an arbitrary figure. The actual media to be used should be indicated—in advertising, for instance, the publications, frequency and size of the ads. If a direct mail campaign, how many shots, to whom, and with what response mechanism. With seminars, how many delegates, how often and where.

Executive summary. It is always useful to include at the beginning or end a short summary of the proposed actions and the reasons behind them.

Tables and charts. These should be used where possible. In particular, a Gantt chart is useful for the timetable.

CHECKLISTS

Two further checklists have been included, one for media relations (editorial publicity) and one for another important element in any public relations campaign, verbal and non–verbal communications. Much of achieving effective public relations depends on individuals, and how they are perceived. For each of the listed criteria, scales of performance should be drawn up and the current achievement should be set against the ideal goals.

TABLE 6
CHECKLIST FOR EDITORIAL PUBLICITY

1. Has the use of editorial publicity been established as an integral part of the operation?

2. Is there a plan of action covering the same period of time as the marketing plan?

3. Have quantified objectives been set for editorial publicity?

4. Are sales staff aware of the value of this form of publicity, and the extent to which they can contribute?

5. Have press lists been drawn up which relate specifically to:
   • the company's activities
   • its markets
   • its products?

6. Has attention been given to the importance of producing press releases tailored to the needs of the particular media concerned?

7. Is photography used wherever possible, and is the same attention given to its creative treatment and production as for press advertising?

8. Are press releases timed to fit in with:
   • editorial press dates
   • the marketing communications campaign?

TABLE 6 *continued*

9. Have good personal relationships been built up between the relevant journalists and the key company staff?

10. Has provision been made:
    • for measuring results
    • for corrective action to be taken, if necessary?

11. Are press cuttings used as a means of evaluation?

12. Are they comprehensive?

13. Are they circulated to personnel who might be interested?

TABLE 7
CHECKLIST OF VERBAL AND NON-VERBAL COMMUNICATIONS

Speaking:

- Style
- Speed
- Clarity
- Accent
- Knowledge and vocabulary
- Enthusiasm
- Visual support

- Rapport
- Clichés
- Listening
- Time
- Program, logic and structure
- Friendliness/familiarity

Non-verbal

- Appearance
- Dress
- Hair
- Clothes
- Body language

- Feel
- Smell
- Job titles
- Mode of travel

THE AUDIT PROCESS

This section addresses the logistical and process requirements of conducting an audit. The topics covered in this section include:

- Staffing the audit team

- Creating an audit project plan

- Laying the groundwork for the audit

- Analyzing audit results

- Sharing audit results

- Writing effective audit reports

- Dealing with resistance to audit recommendations

- Building an ongoing audit program

STAFFING THE AUDIT TEAM

Who conducts the audit is as important in many ways as how the audit is conducted. In fact, the people selected for the audit team will, in large part, determine how the audit is done, how results are analyzed, and how findings are reported. The following list includes general characteristics of effective audit teams for most areas:

- Consists of three to four people.

- Reports to CEO or other senior executive.

- Represents a carefully selected range of skills and experience.

More than four people may be needed for an audit team if data gathering is labor intensive, as when large numbers of customers or employees must be interviewed. However, audit teams of more than six or seven people present problems of maintaining uniformity and communicating audit progress and findings during the course of the evaluation.

Selecting an Audit Team Leader

The audit team leader will play a strong role in shaping both the data gathering and the findings from the audit. The strength of the team leader will also influence the acceptance of the audit, both in terms of enlisting cooperation in the data gathering phase and in securing support for improvement initiatives that grow out of the audit. Because of the importance of this role, care should be taken in selecting the appropriate person for the job. The following qualities are found in successful audit team leaders:

- Has a good relationship with the CEO or with the executive-level sponsor of the audit.

- Is well-liked and well-respected at all levels of the organization, especially in the area to be audited.

- Has good interpersonal skills; can maintain good relationships even in difficult circumstances.

- Has good analytical skills; can assimilate and process large amounts of complex data quickly.

61

- Has some knowledge of the function or area being audited.

- Has extensive knowledge of the type of process being audited.

- Communicates ideas clearly and effectively.

Skills to Be Represented on the Audit Team

Once the team leader has been chosen, audit team members should be selected on the basis of what each can bring to the project. Selection efforts should focus on developing a balanced representation of the following qualities:

- A variety of tenures in the organization, with relative newcomers preferably having experience in other organizations.

- A variety of familiarity with the area (function or site) being audited. Those who are intimately familiar with the area can serve as guides to the less familiar; those who are new to the area can provide objectivity and ask questions that might never be considered by those more involved in the area.

- Considerable familiarity with the type of process being audited. For this reason, many organizations call on people filling roles in similar processes from other parts of the company to work on audit teams.

- Good analytical skills.

- Good interpersonal skills.

- Good facilitation and interviewing skills.

- Good communication skills.

- An understanding of the company's strategy and direction.

CREATING AN AUDIT PROJECT PLAN

Creating an audit project plan accomplishes the following objectives:

- Ensures the allocation of adequate resources, or helps audit team members be prepared to improvise in the face of short resources.

- Ensures the audit is timed so resources are available that may be in high demand.

- Creates clear expectations in the minds of team members about what must be done, and when — especially important when they are not committed to the project full-time.

- Ensures accountability for what must be done, who is responsible for which tasks, and when the audit must be completed.

Financial audits often rely on the Critical Path Method (CPM) of project planning. This method was originally developed by the US Department of Defense during World War II to facilitate the timely completion of weapons development and production. It has since been modified to plan a wide variety of projects. The following outline is a simplification of CPM. It suggests the aspects of a project that should be taken into account during the planning phase.

Critical Path Method

In developing the project plan, audit team members should ask and answer the following questions:

- *What tasks must be performed?*

This list should include the major tasks outlined in the audits, along with subtasks that grow out of those major headings. It should also include any tasks mandated by unique circumstances in the company performing the self-assessment. The audit team may want to brainstorm about tasks that need to be performed, then refine the list to reflect the work priorities of the audit.

- *In what order will the tasks be completed?*

Answering this question should include an analysis of which tasks and sub tasks are dependent on others. Which tasks cannot begin until another has been completed? Which tasks can be done at any time? The audit team may want to place the ordered task on a time line, with start dates, expected duration of the step, and end dates outlined for each task.

- *Who will perform each task?*

Most tasks will be performed by members of the audit team. These assignments should be made by taking the strengths of each team member into consideration, as well as the time availability of each person. Equity of work load should also be taken into account. If tasks are to be assigned to people not on the audit team, those individuals should be included or consulted at this point.

- *What resources will be needed for each step?*

Each task should be analyzed in terms of the personnel, budget, equipment, facilities, support services, and any other resources that will be needed for its completion. The team should assess the availability of all of the resources. Consideration should be given to the task ordering completed earlier. Are some resources subject to competing demands, and therefore difficult to secure at a particular time? How far in advance do arrangements for resources need to be made? Does the task order or time line need to be revised in light of what is known about resource availability?

- *Where is the slack time?*

Slack time is unscheduled time between dependent tasks. Slack provides a degree of flexibility in altering the start dates of subsequent tasks. Slack time signals that a task has a range of possible start dates. It is used to determine the critical path.

- *What is the critical path?*

The critical path in a project is the set of tasks that must be completed in a sequential, chronological order. If any task on the critical path is not completed, all subsequent tasks will be delayed. Delays at any point in the critical path will result in an equivalent delay in the completion of the total project.

Regardless of the method used to develop the project plan, no project, regardless how simple, is ever completed in exact accordance with its plan. However, having a project plan allows the team to gauge its progress, anticipate problems and determine where alternative approaches are needed.

LAYING THE GROUNDWORK FOR THE AUDIT

Once the team has been selected and a project plan developed, the audit leader should prepare those who will be involved in and affected by the audit for the team's visit or for data-gathering. The following steps will help the audit to run more smoothly:

Communicate Executive Support for the Audit

Demonstrating executive support for the audit accomplishes two goals. First, it increases the chances that those involved in the area being audited will cooperate with data gathering efforts. Second, it shows executive support for the area being audited and suggests a commitment to improving the area's performance.

In many companies, the audit is introduced by the executive sponsor of the audit by means of a memo. The memo should explain the purpose of the audit and ask for the support of everyone in the area being audited. This memo is distributed to everyone within the company who will be affected by or involved in the data gathering process. The most effective memos explain how the audit results will be used, reassuring those who will be responding to audit team requests about the motives of the audit. The credibility of such memos is also bolstered when previous audits have been acted upon with positive results.

Make Arrangements with the Area to Be Audited

The audit team leader should check with the appropriate manager in charge of the process or site being audited to arrange for any required on-site visits, interviewing, surveys, focus groups, or written information needed for the audit. The team leader should also explain the purpose, scope, and expected duration of the audit; review the project plan with the manager; and answer any questions the manager has about the audit.

The team leader should also work with the appropriate manager or managers to determine how the audit can be conducted with the least impact on the flow of work. This may include discussions about the timing of the audit, the options for data gathering, the availability of needed data, and possibilities for generating the necessary information quickly and easily. Finding ways to make data collection more efficient and effective is especially important when the audit is part of an ongoing program, rather than an isolated assessment.

Develop a Protocol or Checklist

A protocol or checklist can be used by the audit team to outline the issues that are central to the audit. Written guides can help the leaders of those areas being audited to prepare for the audit. A protocol represents a plan of what the audit team will do to accomplish the objectives of the audit. It is an important tool of the audit, since it not only serves as the audit team's guide to collecting data, but also as a record of the audit procedures completed by the team. In some cases, audit teams may even want to format the checklist in a way that allows them to record their field notes directly on the checklist.

The checklist should include no more than twenty major items, and checklists should be updated with each audit in order to ensure that the appropriate measures are taken. Items where improvement initiatives have been successful should be eliminated from the checklist, with newly identified possibilities for improvement opportunities added.

ANALYZING
AUDIT RESULTS

Discovering gaps between a company's targets and its actual performance is a relatively easy task. Tools are provided to assist audit teams in assessing their performance in a given area. In most cases, more opportunities for improvement will be uncovered by an audit than can be addressed by the resources and energy available. Therefore, one of the most difficult aspects of analyzing the results of an audit lies in determining which opportunities are the most important for managers to pursue.

Because resources and energy for pursuing improvement initiatives are limited, choices must be made about which options are most important. Sometimes these decisions are based on political winds in the company, or on what has worked well in the past, or on personal preferences of top management. However, scarce resources will be used more effectively if allocated to the areas where they will have the greatest impact. Managers must also determine the most effective way to approach initiatives. This section discusses criteria for prioritizing opportunities that grow out of audit findings.

The Novations Strategic Alignment Model

The mid-1980s saw the birth of the "excellence" movement, where many companies tried to achieve excellence in every area of endeavour. Although the movement created an awareness of the need for management improvements, it failed to consider that not all management processes are equal in terms of producing benefits. As a result, leading organizations in today's environment focus on performing well in a few core areas. Knowing what those core areas are depends on a clear vision of the company's strategy.

Strategic thinking about which areas should be improved involves much more than taking an inventory of current capabilities and weaknesses. If it did not, existing capabilities would always determine strategic objectives, and organizational growth and development would come to a halt. To set priorities strategically, companies must decide which improvement opportunities fall in the following categories:

- What to do themselves.

- What to do with someone else.

- What to contract others to do.

- What not to do.

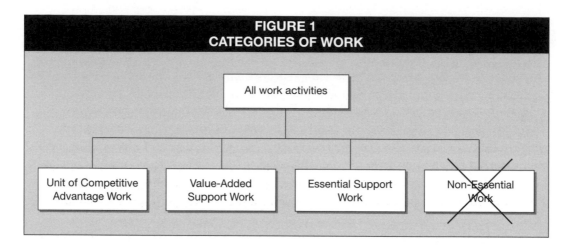

Figure 1 illustrates the four categories of work.

Unit of Competitive Advantage (UCA) Work includes work and capabilities that create distinctiveness for the business in the marketplace.

Value-added Support Work facilitates the accomplishment of the UCA work. For example, a company may have a technology orientation rather than a service orientation, but an effective logistics process may help them to improve their UCA work of providing cutting edge technology.

Essential Support Work neither creates advantage nor facilitates the work that creates advantage, but must be done if businesses are to continue to operate (includes such things as paying taxes, maintaining payroll records, etc.).

Nonessential Work is activity that has lost its usefulness but continues to be done because of tradition.

Despite their sophistication in dealing with other aspects of business, most managers have archaic views of the different types of work. Many of their models for characterizing work have come from a finance or accounting orientation. Accounting terms such as overhead, direct labor, and indirect labor may be useful as a way to report costs, but they provide little understanding about the relative strategic importance of the work. Yet these classifications are frequently used to determine how work is organized and where resources are allocated.

The concept of unit of competitive advantage (UCA) helps to explain why some organizations either emphasize the wrong capabilities or de-emphasize the right capabilities. UCA also explains why some forms of improvement lead to competitive disadvantage, and why some businesses consistently outperform their competitors by gaining greater leverage from their competitive advantages.

A company's UCA includes the critical processes that create distinctiveness within an established strategic direction. It is based on the premise that businesses create competitive advantage when they focus their attention on a few key processes and implement those key processes in world-class fashion. For example, continuous improvement is a popular management program that assumes benefit from any kind of ongoing improvement. Generally speaking, however, continuous improvement program will only create competitive advantage when an organization defines a strategic direction, clarifies strategic objectives, and determines its UCA. These crucial prerequisites tell where continuous improvement efforts should be focused to create maximum leverage. They suggest what kinds of work to improve interdependently, what kinds to improve separately, and what kinds not to waste time on. They even signal when continuous improvement is more likely to create competitive disadvantage rather than competitive advantage.

UCA Initiatives Should Take Priority

Understanding what work falls under which categories requires a clear understanding of the company's strategy. The initiatives resulting from an audit that affect the Unit of Competitive Advantage work processes should clearly have the highest priority among improvement projects. Value-added support initiatives should be second priority, and essential support work should be the third priority. Nonessential work should not be continued.

Once improvement opportunities that will have the greatest impact on the achievement of the company's goals have been identified, the following ideas can be used to lend further insight into how opportunities identified through an audit should be prioritized:

- *Focus on the two or three most important areas.*

Insisting that action be taken on all of the problems uncovered by the audit may overwhelm the people who are responsible for bringing about those changes. Flatter organizations and leaner work forces mean that people are already being asked to do more work with fewer resources and less time. Producing a long list of improvement initiatives may prompt people to dismiss all of them because they don't have time to complete the whole list.

- *Focus on the areas that can be changed.*

Emphasizing problems that are beyond the control of the people who are responsible to work on process improvement only leads to cynicism and a sense of powerlessness. By focusing on things that are within the sphere of influence, accountability for each part of the action plan can be clearly defined.

- *Include as priorities some improvements that can be made quickly.*

Rapid, visible improvement helps build support for more complicated initiatives. Quick improvements also reassure people of management's support for long-term improvement. Seeing immediate improvement helps to build commitment at all levels to the process, and helps build momentum for further change.

- *Emphasize the improvements that seem essential to long-term success.*

Essential improvements may involve sensitive issues or difficult problems, such as deficiencies in fundamental skill levels within the organization or basic strategy issues. These problems are not only difficult and expensive to address, but may also cause a great deal of personal pain or require significant individual adjustment. Nevertheless, long-term improvement requires a commitment to dealing with difficult issues rather than avoiding them.

SHARING AUDIT RESULTS

In most cases, audit results will be presented to various interested people in a feedback meeting. Those in attendance may include members of the executive team, managers who work in the area covered by the audit, the audit team members, and anyone else who is affected by or interested in the results. The meeting should be conducted by members of the audit team. The purpose is to present their findings, and make recommendations for capitalizing on opportunities for improvement.

Conducting Effective Feedback Meetings

The audit team's strategy for the meeting should be to present a clear and simple picture of the current situation as revealed by the audit. This may be a moment of truth for those who have been anticipating the audit results. The feedback meeting for an audit holds both excitement and anxiety: excitement that the future will be bright, and anxiety that shortcomings in individual performance will be highlighted and demands made for personal change. As a result, the meeting must be carefully managed in order to lead to productive change. The following structure is one recommended format for conducting a feedback meeting.

- *Introduce the meeting and preview its agenda.*

This might include an overview of the original intent of the audit, introduction of the audit team, and a brief summary of the meeting's agenda. This step should take no more than five minutes.

- *Present the audit findings.*

Audit findings should summarize the most important points revealed by the data gathered in the audit process. They should be presented separately from the audit recommendations in order to allow people to digest the two parts of the presentation separately. Clearing up misunderstandings about the findings may make the group more accepting of the team's recommendations.

The presentation of the audit findings should take comparatively little time. Audits almost always generate much more data than can be effectively presented or digested in a feedback meeting. The goal of the audit team should be to zero in on the two or three most important points learned from the audit, and present enough supporting data to illustrate those points.

Presenting too much data about audit findings has a number of negative effects. It encourages people to conduct their own analysis of the audit data. To a certain extent, this is a healthy and normal reaction. If others understand the evidence that supports the conclusions drawn by the audit team, they are more likely to accept and own the audit results. Therefore, they will be more committed to the changes brought about by the audit results. However, when people immerse themselves in large amounts of data, they may become victims of "analysis paralysis": they may spend unnecessary time attempting to explain contradictory data, or trying to understand methods used by others to gather data.

- *Present audit recommendations.*

Presenting the audit recommendations should be the central point of the meeting. The recommendations should grow out of the data highlights presented. The audit team should view the recommendations as discussion points for the meeting, rather than as absolute action items.

A common mistake in feedback meetings is to spend most of the meeting on presenting data and recommendations. It is easy for audit team members to become enamored of data they have invested considerable time and energy to collect and analyze. Others in the audience will probably also be interested in the details of the data collected. However, if too much time is spent on discussing the recommendations, the meeting will end before a commitment to action has been made.

- *Ask others to react to the data.*

The reactions of top management and those responsible for implementing audit recommendations will determine the ultimate value of the audit data. Therefore, the feedback meeting is a good time to resolve questions or problems with the findings and recommendations as they have been presented. If resistance to the audit findings is not resolved in the feedback meeting, opportunities for improvement may be lost.

Those attending the meeting may offer their opinions willingly. If not, the audit team members should ask the others in the room for their reaction to what has been presented.

- *Develop preliminary action plans.*

The detailed action plans should grow out of the recommendations made by the audit team. They should specifically address the question of who should do what by when. Formal accountability mechanisms should be established before the end of the meeting, such as the scheduling of subsequent meetings or follow-up check points.

WRITING EFFECTIVE AUDIT REPORTS

There are three fundamental purposes for writing a formal report at the conclusion of an audit:

- An audit report may be a stand-alone summary of the audit. This approach is not recommended, inasmuch as the report is likely to be filed away, making the probability of action unlikely.

- The report may supplement a feedback meeting, providing those in attendance with documentation and an outline to follow.

- The report should also serve as a baseline document to make measurement of performance improvement possible in future audits.

Because the written report is the most enduring part of the audit presentation, it should be well written and easy to understand. The following tips will lead to the preparation of effective written audit reports.

Focus on a Few Key Points

The audit presentation should focus on the two or three most important findings. It is impossible to present all of the data gathered in the audit to those who were not on the audit team. It is also not advisable to present every detail of the data. The audit team members should trust their own judgment about what the highlights of the study were, and present enough data to support that judgment. For each of the major findings, the team may want to include the following information:

- What is the problem?

- Why does it exist?

- What happens if the problem is not fixed:

  — in the short term?

  — in the long term?

- Recommend solutions.

- Outline expected benefits.

Prepare an Outline Before Writing the First Draft

A good outline ensures that the logic of the report is clear, and that ideas proceed in an order that makes sense. The following outline provides one approach that works effectively.

Background

This section should establish the framework for the audit in terms of:

- Providing a brief discussion of the overall purpose of the audit.

- Identifying the role of the audit team in the overall process.

- Establishing the limitations of the audit methodology to ensure that others utilize the results provided in the report appropriately.

Objectives

This section should identify specific objectives of the audit in terms of types of information the team was expected to generate.

Methodology

The methodology section should describe the mechanics of the audit and include the following information:

- Types of assessment used (survey, interviews, focus groups, etc.).

- Data sources, or the sample groups for each of the types of assessment used.

- Time frame during which the audit was conducted.

- Other pertinent details about how the audit was conducted.

Findings

This section is designed to provide others with a review of the "facts" that came out of the audit. Except in cases where an audit checks regulatory compliance, only the most significant findings should be discussed in any detail in the report. This section should also include briefly presented data supporting the findings.

Conclusions

This section should report the audit team's interpretation of what the facts of the audit mean in light of the objectives stated at the outset of the audit.

Recommendations

This section includes suggestions from the audit team on how to close the performance gaps identified in the audit. The degree of specificity to be included in the audit report will vary from company to company and audit to audit.

Appendix

This portion of the formal report should include any of the following items that are relevant to the audit:

- A copy of any questionnaires or survey instruments used in the audit.

- A summary of the data gathered in the course of the audit.

- Recommendations for subsequent audits based on the team's experience.

Present Audit Findings Accurately

Those who read the report will no doubt be somewhat familiar with the area covered by the audit. They may notice discrepancies between what they know about the subject and what is reported in the written document. Spotting one inaccuracy may lead the readers to discredit all of the findings, conclusions and recommendations. Audit team members should be careful to report data as it was actually generated, and to describe the impact of the findings accurately.

Use Clear, Concise Language

Every statement included in the report should be based on sound evidence developed or reviewed during the audit. Whatever is said must be supported or supportable. Speculation should be avoided. Generalities and vague reporting will only confuse and mislead those that the report should influence or inform. For example, a report using the terms some, a few, or not all can leave the reader confused about the significance of the finding. Specific quantities should be used, such as, "of the ten samples taken, two were found to be…", "Three of five respondents said that…", and so on. Statements should be qualified as needed, and any unconfirmed data or information should be identified as such.

Ideas or sentences that do not amplify the central theme should be eliminated. The report should not identify individuals or highlight the mistakes of individuals.

Use Good Grammar and Style

Basic grammar and style rules should be followed in writing the text. Below are some examples:

- Avoid extreme terms, such as alarming, deplorable, gross negligence, etc.

- Avoid using redundant or lengthy phrases, such as calling something an emergency situation when the word emergency alone will do.

- Avoid verbs camouflaged as nouns or adjectives. For example, use "the new procedure will reduce error entries," rather than "The new procedure will accomplish a reduction of error entries."

- Avoid indirect expressions where possible. For example, "Many instances of poor management were found," is more direct than saying, "There were many instances of poor judgment found."

- Use short, familiar words. Use words that are easily understandable to everyone and that convey the message concisely.

- Keep sentences short. Most writing experts suggest that an average sentence should be between 15 and 18 words. Packing too many ideas into a single sentence confuses and tires readers.

The audit team should provide enough background information in the report so that the reader clearly understands who conducted the audit and what the audit did or did not include. The purpose of the report as well as the purpose and scope of the audit should also be described in a manner that enables the reader to know why the report was written and who should take corrective action.

Timing of the Report

The timing of audit reports is critical to the overall reporting process and must be carefully thought out. In many cases, a written draft of the audit report is prepared one to three weeks before the feedback meeting. This draft then goes through a review and another report is prepared in time for the team's presentation. A final report may be completed after the feedback session has been held in order to record changes resulting from that meeting.

DEALING WITH RESISTANCE TO RECOMMENDATIONS

Most audit teams feel that if they can present their ideas clearly and logically, and have the best interests of the company or department at heart, managers will accept the recommendations made as part of the audit and follow the team's recommendations. Many people who have worked in organizations, however, find that no matter how reasonably recommendations are presented, they are all too often not implemented.

Implementation usually fails because it requires people to change their ways of working. That change requires a great deal of effort, energy, and risk; therefore, change is usually resisted. Resistance is an emotional process; people may embrace recommendations based on their logic, but fail to implement them because of the emotional resistance to the personal change involved. Resistance is a predictable, natural, and necessary part of the learning process. Although resistance may cause audit team members to feel they have missed the mark in terms of the recommendations they have made, it actually often signals accuracy in having interpreted the organization's needs. By dealing with the resistance directly, audit teams can work through barriers to implementing process improvements.

What Are the Signs of Resistance?

In many cases, resistance may be expressed directly. Direct objections to recommendations are relatively easy to address, inasmuch as they can be discussed and resolved. When recommendations are being presented, team members should stop frequently to allow those who are listening to the report to voice any objections or disagreements. Those who are presenting the data should be careful not to become defensive or to punish those who express reservations about the recommendations. It is impossible to deal with objections unless they are voiced; therefore, the audit team should welcome the expression of objections or differences of opinion. The following tips may be used for surfacing and dealing with direct resistance:

• Provide many opportunities for others to express their concerns.

• Carefully clarify any confusing concerns.

• Deal with important or easy concerns immediately. Defer the remainder.

• Summarize the concerns before moving on. Show that concerns have been heard.

- It may even be helpful to list concerns on a flip chart or blackboard.

If direct resistance continues, the following steps may be necessary:

- Talk about the differences of opinion.

- Voice concern and support for negotiating a resolution.

- Avoid struggles for control of the situation.

Dealing with Indirect Resistance

In other cases, resistance may be subtle and elusive. Indirect resistance is difficult to identify and deal with because its manifestations seem logical. People who are experiencing indirect resistance may feel that they are "getting the run around." Many different forms of resistance may manifest themselves in a single meeting:

- Request for more detail.

- Providing too much detail in response to questions.

- Complaining that there isn't enough time to implement recommendations.

- Claiming that the recommendations are impractical.

- Attacking those who propose improvement initiatives.

- Acting confused.

- Responding with silence.

- Intellectualizing about the data.

- Moralizing that problems wouldn't exist if it weren't for "those people".

- Agreeing to implement recommendations with no intention of acting on them.

- Asking questions about methodology.

- Arguing that previous problems have resolved themselves.

- Focusing on solutions before findings are fully understood.

Almost any of these responses is legitimate in moderate amounts. For example, members of the group may have concerns about the audit's methodology that should be considered. Managers may realistically wonder where they will find the time to implement recommendations. However, if refusal to act on recommendations persists once legitimate concerns have been addressed, then the audit team is probably facing indirect resistance.

Many models used in sales training provide recommendations for overcoming resistance. These methods suggest the use of data and logical arguments to win the point and convince the other person to buy whatever is being sold. These models work well for direct resistance. However, indirect resistance is normally based on feelings rather than logic. Therefore, the only way to truly overcome resistance is to deal with the emotional processes that cause it to happen in the first place. It is almost impossible to talk people out of the way they feel.

Feelings pass and change when they are expressed directly. A key skill for audit teams that are attempting to implement recommendations is to ask the people who are presenting resistance to put directly into words what they are experiencing. The most effective way to make this happen is for the audit team members to address directly what is happening in the situation. The following keys provide help in surfacing and dealing with indirect resistance.

- *Work once or twice with the person's concern, even when it feels as if he or she is resisting recommendations.*

By attempting to work with the problem stated by the person raising a concern, audit team members can determine whether the concern is legitimate or whether it is an excuse for not taking action. If the issues raised are legitimate, the person should show some willingness to discuss and resolve them. If the issues are manifestations of indirect resistance, the person will probably respond with other forms of resistance.

- *Identify the form the resistance is taking.*

Paying attention to the dynamics of a discussion can provide important clues as to whether or not a person is resisting recommendations. If a person is consistently distancing him or herself from those who are presenting the audit findings, using gestures or postures that suggest tension or discomfort, while at the same time presenting arguments for why the recommendations presented are inappropriate, it is probably a sign of resistance. The non-verbal responses of the presenters may also signal the onset of resistance. If presenters feel that they are suppressing negative feelings or becoming bored or irritated, it may be further evidence that the client is resisting.

Once presenters become aware of the resistance, the next step is to put it into words. This is best done by using neutral, everyday language. The skill is to describe the form of the resistance in a way that encourages the person to make a more direct statement of the reservation he or she is experiencing.

One general rule for stating what type of resistance is being manifested is to phrase the statement in common, non-threatening language. Statements should be made in the same tone and language that would be used to address a problem with a spouse or close friend. The statement should be made with as little evaluation as possible; it is the presenter's observation about what is happening in the situation.

A second general rule for surfacing indirect resistance involves not talking for a couple of moments after the presenter has stated what he or she has observed. There may be a temptation to elaborate on the observation, or to support it with evidence. However, continuing the statement will reduce the tension in the situation. Without tension, the person who is resisting feels no discomfort, and is unlikely to address the issue directly. Moreover, elaborating on the original statement may increase the other person's defensiveness and reduce the chances of solving the problem.

If stating the problem in direct, non-punishing terms fails to bring the resistance out into the open, there may be little more the audit team can do to overcome the indirect resistance. The best strategy in this case is to avoid resisting the resistance. Team members should support the person who is resisting and proceed with the implementation of recommendations to the extent possible.

BUILDING AN ONGOING AUDIT PROGRAM

As the pace of change increases, and as organization leaders become more and more committed to continuously improving their effectiveness and efficiency, audits of all types of processes will become more common. The most effective companies will establish program of ongoing audits, whereby a number of goals can be accomplished:

- Performance improvements can be measured over time.

- Important changes in the company's environment can be systematically monitored.

- Managers can make a habit of change and improvement, rather than resisting it.

- Those areas that are of highest importance to the company can be routinely improved.

- Processes can be modified to be in alignment with changes in strategy or in the environment.

As with all management techniques, however, an enduring program of ongoing audits requires that audits become integrated into the overall management system. The following guidelines are keys to weaving audits into the fabric of day-to-day operations.

Establish Support for Ongoing Audits

While support for audits begins at the executive level, ownership for the audit process must be felt throughout the organization if an ongoing program is to be successful. The following actions will help to broaden support for the audit process, while ensuring greater benefit from the audit.

- *Share the results of the audit with everyone throughout the organization.*

By keeping others informed about the results of an audit, managers reassure those who participate in and are affected by the audit of the integrity of the process. Employees sometimes become suspicious of probing investigators; they may have doubts about how the information will be used, or whether the information will be used. By sharing audit results, managers make an implicit commitment to improving the processes that have been evaluated.

- *Act on the audit results.*

Questions will be raised about continuing audits if early assessments bear no fruits. Failing to act on performance gaps that are identified leads to cynicism and lack of trust among those who work with the problems daily. On the other hand, improving a process can create the momentum that comes from accomplishment. Committing resources and attention to the improvement opportunities revealed by an audit also shows management commitment to the improvement process.

- *Let others know when performance has improved.*

Communicating the positive results from an audit is one way of rewarding the people who contributed to that improvement. It also builds faith in the effectiveness of the audit process. Moreover, showing that performance has improved is another means of reassuring people of a commitment to the improvement process.

- *Reward people for their part in improvements.*

Increasing efficiency and effectiveness can often be a threatening experience for those who are involved in a work process. Improving the way resources are used often means eliminating the need for some of the people who have been involved in the process. Although flatter, leaner organizations often preclude the possibility of offering promotions, managers should nevertheless attempt to ensure that people who contribute to performance improvement find their own situations better rather than worse as a result.

Rewards for helping to close performance gaps may span a range from thanking people for their efforts to planning a group celebration to offering bonuses or pay increases for improvement. Rewards are especially meaningful when people are allowed to suggest what rewards they would like for their contribution. This may provide managers with new ideas for rewards that may be less costly to the organization than financial recognition.

- *Involve a wide variety of people in the audit process.*

People can be involved in the audit process in many ways. By involving people from a broad spectrum, more people learn about audit techniques and results, thus spreading commitment to the audit process throughout the organization. By involving many people in the data-gathering process, employees feel that action plans growing out of the audit were a result of their input. Excluding people from the data-gathering phase usually reduces the feeling of ownership for the results, thus making people feel as if initiatives are being imposed on them. By the same token, involving a broad range of people in the development of action plans expands ownership for the plans and allows for the generation of more ideas.

Implementing A Public Relations Audit: Questions And Checklists

This section of the Public Relations Audit comprises a series of questions based on the nine steps in Part 1. These questions have been designed to help you plan and implement your audit in a straightforward and practical manner, covering all the relevant parts of the audit in the correct sequence.

Nine steps for auditing a company's public relations

- Step 1 The Internal Image Audit
- Step 2 The Consultancy Audit
- Step 3 Choosing a Consultancy
- Step 4 Assessing Staff Skills and Competencies
- Step 5 Public Relations Publics Audit
- Step 6 Selecting the Media
- Step 7 Good Media Relations
- Step 8 Public Relations Evaluation
- Step 9 The Ten-Point Public Relations Plan

Note: Before you look at the questions below, do read the audit introduction and What Are We Doing Now? Additionally, useful background information is given for each step before the questions themselves are listed, and two further checklists are provided at the end of the audit.

THE INTERNAL IMAGE AUDIT

BACKGROUND INFORMATION

Examining an organization's image requires careful evaluation of all deliberate and active sources of publicity (i.e. advertising, direct mail, exhibitions), outside message sources (i.e. third-party endorsement), the impression employees give (i.e. receptionist right up to the chief executive), and all other passive message sources (i.e. any factor that contributes to the public's perception – office decor and tidiness, job titles, letter headings, etc.).

The first task is putting together a checklist of the message sources that will be used for the audit. Each message source needs to be evaluated as to whether is creates a favorable, neutral, or unfavorable impression. An action program can be put into place for those messages that are categorized as unfavorable followed by an examination of neutral message sources, and then finally those considered favorable can then be looked at for further improvement.

Five aspects of internal auditing need to be considered.

1. The External Image Audit.

2. The Corporate Personality.

3. Organizing for Public Relations.

4. Internal/External Services.

5. Using and Auditing a Consultancy.

In the "Questions" section below is a set of questions for internal image auditing.

QUESTIONS

- Have you produced a checklist of message sources to be used for the internal image audit?

- Does the checklist include:

  ❏ active message sources (promotional)

  ❏ outside message sources

  ❏ people message sources

  ❏ passive message sources?

Note: Table 1, Step 1 of Part 1 provides a full listing of potential message sources.

- Has a small project team of roughly three senior people been assembled?

- Has the team reached a consensus on whether any given message source is creating a favorable, neutral, or unfavorable impression?

1. *The External Image Audit*

- Once the internal image audit has been run, are you planning to run through the same procedure with a group of people from outside the organization (e.g. customers)?

- To ensure all important message sources are included, do you intend to use a focus group discussion to uncover any further criteria that should be added to the audit?

- Have you considered engaging the services of an outside market research company at this stage?

- If considerable doubt is uncovered regarding the perception of message sources by the focus group, would you consider extending the study to quantitative research?

2. *The Corporate Personality*

- Does your corporate image come out of the company's mission statement?

- Which of the following attributes are associated with your company name:
  - ❏ innovative, proactive, creative
  - ❏ market leader, profitable
  - ❏ well managed, reliable, safe, responsible
  - ❏ international, British, Japanese, or any other nationality
  - ❏ diversified, specialist
  - ❏ authoritative, technical leader, expert
  - ❏ honest, decent, truthful
  - ❏ high quality, value for money
  - ❏ friendly, responsive, caring
  - ❏ excellent in pre- and post-sales service?

3. Organizing for Public Relations

- As the first and most important step in organizing public relations, does your company PR function correctly fit within the management structure and report directly to the CEO?

Note: Figure 5, Step 1 of Part 1 shows how the public relations function currently fits with other management functions. It disputes the common practice of making PR part of the marketing team as PR has an important contribution to make to other functions like finance and human resources, and to the business as a whole.

4. Internal/External Services

- Has there been an assessment as to what extent various specialized PR functions should be outsourced?

Note: Table 2, Step 1 of Part 1 provides a list of some of the main outside PR services available.

- In particular, has consideration been given to using a public relations consultancy?

When considering using a public relations consultancy, three points need to be looked at:
- strengths
- weaknesses, and
- why, if and when.

Strengths

- Have you considered the following strengths of a public relations consultancy:
  - ❏ professionalism
  - ❏ objectivity
  - ❏ credibility
  - ❏ expandable service?

Weaknesses

- Have you also considered the following possible weaknesses of a public relations consultancy:
  - ❏ limited time
  - ❏ superficial

❏ expensive

❏ staff turnover?

Why, if and when

- At the very least, have you considered the benefits to be gained from getting outside advice on setting down the objectives and a plan of action?

- In preparation for using a public relations consultancy for some advice, have you:

  ❏ written down the activities which need to be undertaken in order to achieve the public relations objectives

  ❏ talked to one or two consultancies in order to find out in what ways they would feel able to contribute?

5. Using and Auditing a Consultancy

- In order to obtain good value for money along with first-class service and performance from a public relations consultancy, are you aware that:

  ❏ the consultancy must receive adequate information

  ❏ there must be a method of evaluating the service provided (i.e. an audit)?

As regards receiving adequate information, three aspects need to be considered:
- briefing
- the background brief, and
- the tactical brief.

Briefing

- If you already have a relationship with a consultancy and you feel there is room for improvement, are you actually confident that everything has been done to enable the consultancy to perform well?

- If it is a new relationship, have you ensured that all personnel who will have any involvement with the account are thoroughly familiar with the nature of your business, its products and markets, and its objectives?

The background brief

- Have you held a one- or two-day seminar with the consultancy, presented by senior specialists from your company?

- If so, have all the following topics been included:

  ❏ objectives (e.g. short- and long-term objectives for the business, market share, sales, research and development)

  ❏ external factors (i.e. anticipated factors outside the control of the company which may affect its objectives)

  ❏ internal factors (as the result of a SWOT analysis – strengths, weaknesses, opportunities and threats)

  ❏ the market (market size, perceptions, etc.)

  ❏ product portfolio (familiarity with the entire product range)

  ❏ competition (a comparison of competitors' products with your own company's products)

  ❏ pricing strategy (basis of pricing and relationship with competitive prices)

  ❏ service (pre-sales, sales and after-sales service).

Note: Much of this information will be of a confidential and sensitive nature, but will be necessary if your company and the consultancy are to work together efficiently. Having put this information together initially, provision must be made for periodic updates.

The tactical brief

- Are you aware that, in addition to the background brief, every job undertaken by the consultancy will require a tactical brief?

- Are you also aware that a tactical brief should be put in writing and approved by any senior management who will wish to have a say in the final outcome?

Having completed the questions in Step 1, you will now need to consider how to effectively assess a public relation consultancy's performance. Extensive information for this is provided in Step 2 of Part 1. A brief list of appropriate audit questions follows an outline of this step.

THE CONSULTANCY AUDIT

BACKGROUND INFORMATION

One well tested and effective method of assessing a public relations consultancy's performance is to set up a structured annual consultancy audit. This requires drawing up a list of criteria against which the consultancy's performance will be judged and which then form the basis of an annual review meeting.

A meeting of key personnel from both the consultancy and client permits a frank exchange of views. Against the client's appraisal, the consultancy should be permitted the opportunity to give explanations. Finally, an agreement can be reached as to the best course of action.

In the "Questions" section below you will find a set of questions that will help you to establish a regular consultancy audit.

QUESTIONS

* Have you decided to set up a structured consultancy audit?

* How frequently will these audits be held?

* Have you drawn up a list of criteria against which the consultancy's performance can be judged?

Note: A suggested audit checklist containing 10 different criteria is provided on page 24 of Step 2 in Part 1.

* How will the consultancy's performance against each criterion be rated:

  ❏ semantically (i.e. 'very good', 'average' or 'completely unacceptable')

  ❏ arithmetically (marks out of 5 or 10)?

* Will you arrange a meeting with the consultancy to discuss the outcome of the audit and jointly agree any course of action?

Having looked into the setting up of a regular consultancy audit, you will now need to consider how to choose the best consultancy to work with your company. Details for this are provided in Step 3 of Part 1. A brief list of appropriate audit questions follows an outline of this step.

CHOOSING A CONSULTANCY

BACKGROUND INFORMATION

There is a three-stage approach to finding the best public relations consultancy for your company involving the following.

1. Coarse screening.

2. Fine screening.

3. The pitch.

In the "Questions" section below you will find a set of questions that will take you through this three-stage operation.

QUESTIONS

1. Coarse screening

- Have you drawn up a consultancy specification outlining all the services required along with the nature of the organization (size, location, number of clients, staff specializations, etc.)?

- Have you compiled a list of 12 candidate consultancies?

Note: Listings of public relations consultancies are to be found in directories such as *Hollis Press and Public Relations Annual* and *Public Relations Consultants Association Yearbook*.

- In putting together a list of candidate consultancies, have you avoided those handling a competitive account?

- Does the list include consultancies that are well acquainted with the same markets and publics, and known to have very effective public relations?

- Has a letter been sent to the CEO of each consultancy, in confidence, asking whether or not they would feel able to handle your company as a new client and, if so, to write giving such details as they think appropriate?

- In putting together this mailing to the CEOs, was the specification included?

- As a result of the response received from these letters, has a shortlist of three consultancies been drawn up?

- In the course of this screening stage, have the following been consulted:
  - ❏ colleagues
  - ❏ contacts
  - ❏ any existing file of propositions sent in cold over the previous year
  - ❏ two or three friendly journalists?

2. Fine screening

- Has a letter been sent to the three shortlisted candidates indicating your wish to proceed further?

- Has a visit to each consultancy been arranged in order to do a 'credentials presentation' (i.e. the consultancy will present examples of relevant campaigns)?

- Has personal contact been made with all the clients involved in these campaigns to get a view from their side?

- Has each consultancy paid you a visit in order to see how they would relate to you and your colleagues on 'home ground'?

3. The pitch

- Has each of the three candidate consultancies been given a carefully prepared written brief outlining what would be required of them if they were to win the account?

- Have they also been given the opportunity to ask for elaboration on any points?

- Have they been allowed a reasonable period of time in which to prepare, in effect, an outline communications plan?

- Has it been agreed whether or not a fee will be paid for this work?

- When the communications plan is presented, is the presentation team the one that is going to work on the account?

- Has consideration been given to whether or not you and your colleagues would enjoy working with them?

- Rather than state what your budget is, have you asked each consultancy to advise you on the budget once they have had the briefing?

Having chosen your public relations consultancy, the next step of the audit involves assessing your staff skills and competencies. Extensive information for this is provided in Step 4 of Part 1. A brief list of appropriate audit questions follows an outline of this step.

ASSESSING STAFF SKILLS
AND COMPETENCIES

BACKGROUND INFORMATION

Today, a public relations executive needs to have an all-round capability in every form of communications. There are certainly many elements of public relations practice that can be taught, but a major increase has been detected in the field of training.

The Institute of Public Relations and the Public Relations Consultants Association in the UK have jointly produced the 'Public Relations Education and Training Matrix' which has been designed as a basis for:

- self-assessment of training needs and career development

- appraisal of employees' skills and their development needs, and

- evaluation of training and education course suitability.

The matrix has four categories:

- knowledge

- business skills

- public relations skills – counselling and planning, and

- public relations skills – implementation.

The matrix also has five different stages of knowledge skills or experience.

In the "Questions" section below you will find a set of questions to assist in the assessment of staff skills and competencies.

QUESTIONS

- Have your staff been educated in the elements of public research practice such as:
  - ❏ research into target audiences
  - ❏ planning and budgeting
  - ❏ inter- and intra-media comparisons
  - ❏ typography?

- Have you used the Public Relations Education and Training Matrix to assess the training needs and career development of your public relations staff?

• Have you used the matrix to appraise employees' skills and their development needs?

• Have you also used the matrix to evaluate training and education course suitability?

Having completed the questions in Step 4, you will now need to consider what is involved in carrying out a public relations publics audit. Details of this are provided in Step 5 of Part 1. A brief list of appropriate audit questions follows an outline of this step.

PUBLIC RELATIONS PUBLICS AUDIT

BACKGROUND INFORMATION

The 'publics' are the many groups of people whose opinion is of importance to an organization. Occasionally they are referred to as the stakeholders, and they are the target audiences for any public relations campaign and, as such, will be an intrinsic part of it.

There are four publics that need to be looked at.

1. Marketing publics (including everyone who makes up the decision-making unit – DMU).

2. Personnel or human resources publics.

3. Financial publics.

4. Corporate publics.

In the "Questions" section below you will find a set of questions examining each of the groups.

QUESTIONS

1. Marketing publics

- In consumer marketing, has consideration been given to the various members of a family that might be involved in the purchasing decision?

- In business to business marketing, have all the following people been considered as part of the DMU:

  ❏ the individual/people who specify that a product or service is required

  ❏ the people who influence this requirement

  ❏ those in authority (for a major purchase, the entire board of directors)

  ❏ the purchasing department executives who have to undertake the transaction?

- Has consideration been given to the 'gatekeeper' – anyone in a position to intercept a selling message, such as a secretary or receptionist?

- When looking at users, has consideration been given to the fact that this might be just one person or it may be hundreds?

- For other public relations publics, has consideration also been given to the many individuals to be influenced behind one single target audience?

- To recap, have the following six categories of individuals been allowed for:
  - ❏ specifier
  - ❏ influencer
  - ❏ authorizer
  - ❏ buyer
  - ❏ gatekeeper
  - ❏ user?

- In marketing publics, has special note been taken of competitors and has consideration been given as to whether any special campaign is required?

- Has the final category in the marketing arena – third-party audiences – been considered?

- Which of the following third-party audiences have been thought about:
  - ❏ the retailer (including all shop assistants and retail staff)
  - ❏ business partners
  - ❏ agents
  - ❏ distributors
  - ❏ trade associations?

2. Personnel or human resources publics

- When considering employees, have the following also been included:
  - ❏ hired-in staff
  - ❏ employees' families
  - ❏ past employees
  - ❏ future employees
  - ❏ employee organizations (e.g. trade unions)?

- Have you carried out an internal attitude audit to specify the individual groups?

- If you have, did it include:
  - ❏ CEO
  - ❏ directors
  - ❏ management
  - ❏ salespeople
  - ❏ service staff
  - ❏ reception
  - ❏ telephonists
  - ❏ secretaries
  - ❏ drivers
  - ❏ operatives
  - ❏ security
  - ❏ canteen
  - ❏ cleaners?

- Under the human resources umbrella, have the local community and local government also been considered?

- Have local opinion formers and decision makers been included, such as:
  - ❏ doctors
  - ❏ police
  - ❏ solicitors
  - ❏ teachers
  - ❏ club leaders
  - ❏ the clergy
  - ❏ councilors
  - ❏ local authority staff
  - ❏ local media?

3. *Financial publics*

- In addition to shareholders, have potential shareholders and past shareholders been included?

- Has consideration been given to whether these groups have DMUs?

- Have the following DMUs been included:
  - ❏ stockbrokers
  - ❏ financial analysts
  - ❏ banks
  - ❏ accountancy practices
  - ❏ other intermediaries
  - ❏ financial media?

4. Corporate publics

- In looking at corporate publics, has provision been made for all:
  - ❏ elected representatives
  - ❏ prospective candidates
  - ❏ civil servants in the ministries?

- If action on a national basis is required, have regional bodies such as the European Union and international bodies been included?

- Do any of these other groups apply:
  - ❏ employers' professional and trade associations
  - ❏ special-interest groups
  - ❏ opinion formers?

Having ensured that the target audience is comprehensive and complete, attention must turn to selecting your media channels. Information for this is provided in Step 6 of Part 1. A brief list of appropriate audit questions follows an outline of this step.

Step **6**

SELECTING THE MEDIA

BACKGROUND INFORMATION

As media channels have their own limitations, it is usually necessary to employ a combination or 'media mix' in order to communicate effectively.

When selecting your media channels, various points need to be considered.

1. Media strengths and weaknesses.

2. The media mix.

3. Inter-media comparisons.

4. Other choices in media.

In the "Questions" section below you will find a set of questions that will take you through these various aspects involved in media selection.

QUESTIONS

1. Media strengths and weaknesses

The strengths and weaknesses of the media need to be looked at in terms of:

- editorial publicity

- press advertising

- exhibitions

- direct mail

- television advertising

- radio advertising

- cinema

- posters, and

- telemarketing.

Editorial publicity

- Are you aware that news stories or feature articles are far more credible than advertisements in the same publication for the following reasons:
  - ❏ they have the implied endorsement of the publication
  - ❏ there are up to five times the number of readers
  - ❏ it is free?

- On the downside, are you aware that:
  - ❏ there is no control over whether or not the story will ever appear
  - ❏ if it does appear, there is no control over whether the story will be complimentary or accurate
  - ❏ it will only appear once?

Press advertising

- Are you aware that with press advertising, an ad is fully controllable in terms of:
  - ❏ when it appears
  - ❏ where it appears
  - ❏ what it says
  - ❏ how large it is
  - ❏ when it should be repeated?

- On the downside though, have you considered that advertising:
  - ❏ is expensive
  - ❏ has fewer readers
  - ❏ is obviously biased?

Exhibitions

- Have you ever considered the cost effectiveness of an exhibition in terms of:
  - ❏ the number of personal one-to-one interviews that can be achieved in a day
  - ❏ the fact that the buyer is calling on the seller requesting information
  - ❏ the opportunity to demonstrate products
  - ❏ the opportunity to get feedback on a product's operation and application
  - ❏ the corporate image value?

- Have you also considered the following drawbacks of exhibitions:

  ❏ high basic cost

  ❏ internal disruption prior, during and after the event

  ❏ the number and quality of visitors may be disappointing?

Direct mail

- Have you considered the strengths of direct mail, including:

  ❏ messages can be sent directly to the target audience

  ❏ there is wide scope for creative opportunity (endless materials can be used and sensory effects achieved)

  ❏ it has a good response capability?

- Have you also considered the following weakness of direct mail:

  ❏ inaccuracy of mailing databases

  ❏ the difficulty of defining with accuracy the members of the decision-making units (DMUs)

  ❏ the problems of imagery (i.e. rubbish mailing)?

Television advertising

- Have you considered the high-impact, mass communication opportunity offered by television advertising?

- Have you also considered the potentially vast wastage and extremely high cost of it?

Radio advertising

- In comparing radio advertising with television advertising, have you thought about:

  ❏ the easier segmentation of radio

  ❏ the great value radio advertising has for local community campaigns

  ❏ radio costs less

  ❏ radio has less of an impact?

Cinema

- Have you considered cinema advertising for precisely focusing on two age groups – teens and forties?

- However, are you aware that it is not a suitable medium for a public relations campaign?

Posters

- Did you know that this is a very precise medium for consumer marketing, provided that the message is simple?

- Are you aware that posters have little application in public relations other than in special circumstances (e.g. exhibition halls, airports, railway stations)?

Telemarketing

- Have you considered using telemarketing as a follow-up system on direct mail campaigns (together known as direct marketing)?

- Are you aware of the strengths of telemarketing in terms of:
  - ❑ making personal contact with speed and impact
  - ❑ fixing appointments
  - ❑ gaining data and responses to support marketing research programs?

2. The media mix

- Do you understand the concept of a 'media mix' in terms of selecting by methodical analysis an optimum combination of media categories to achieve the desired effect?

3. Inter-media comparisons

- Have you used available data to make a comparative judgement on an effective media mix?

- Due to the frequent scarcity of data or information for this judgment, have you created some form of logical grid?

- Within the grid, have you evaluated each possible medium and given it a comparative rating?

Note: An example of a typical grid is provided in Figure 6, Step 6 of Part 1.

The following 12 factors should be taken into account when planning a public relations campaign:

- audience
- impact
- message
- coverage and penetration
- negative characteristics
- positive characteristics
- cost
- speed
- complexity and convenience
- feedback
- creative scope
- data availability.

Audience

- Are you aware that the total size of a target audience or market segment and all the people comprising it must be the starting point for any media choice?

- Are you also aware of the following limits:
    - ❑ up to 10, there is no room for more than personal contact
    - ❑ up to 100, the situation hardly changes
    - ❑ up to 1000, personal contact must become selective and so you can add direct mail, specialized press advertising, editorial publicity, literature, sponsored films, local demonstrations and telephone calls
    - ❑ at 10,000, personal contact falls away and press advertising and other non-personal media take over (i.e. public exhibitions, editorial backup)
    - ❑ at 100,000, you move into mass media (i.e. television, radio, national newspapers and posters)?

Note: Figure 7, Step 6 of Part 1 indicates how media choice varies with audience size.

Impact

- Are you aware that the extent to which a promotion message is transmitted, received, stored, and is able to be recalled is vital?

- Are you aware of the intrinsic impact potential of each medium as follows:
  - ❏ a medium which facilitates two-way communication is top of the list (e.g. personal contacts, exhibitions, demonstrations, telephone calls)
  - ❏ in addition, direct mail, editorial publicity, sponsored film and literature can all expect to have high impact potential
  - ❏ press advertising performs least well in achieving impact
  - ❏ television has a high impact potential?

Message

- Have you considered the nature of the message?

- Is it simple or is it a reminder?

- Is it:
  - ❏ complex
  - ❏ technical
  - ❏ innovative?

Coverage and penetration

- As regards the breadth of a medium's capability, have you ascertained what proportion of the target audience is covered by readership as opposed to circulation?

- Have you found a medium with an in-depth coverage of around 80 percent?

- As regards penetration, have you considered those media which are known by long-standing practice to penetrate decision-making units (DMUs) even where the people involved cannot be identified?

Negative characteristics

- Have you considered that some people resent some advertising and whether it will be counterproductive?

- Are you aware that the following media are often unpopular or viewed as intrusive in the UK:
  - ❏ advertising message on the telephone
  - ❏ salespeople at the front door

❑ salespeople on the street corner

❑ loose inserts

❑ direct mail which is too expensive or repetitive

❑ radio and television commercials?

Positive characteristics

- Does one particular medium have an added plus that puts it ahead of the rest (e.g. an ad in a very prestigious publication which benefits from the other ads around it)?

Cost

- Have you considered the two costs involved – the total capital investment and the cost per contact – as well as the price of the medium?

- Do you plan to engage in some aggressive media buying and have you set a target discount rate of 10 percent?

Speed

- Do you need to get a message across very quickly and so are considering television, radio, newspapers or direct mail?

- If you are waiting for an appropriate trade fair to take place, may this be too long a wait for activating consumer/customer behavior?

Complexity and convenience

- Have you considered the amount of effort required to service each medium in relation to the income and aggravation involved?

Feedback

- If you want to receive direct feedback, will you consider all the face-to-face media along with direct mail and editorial publicity?

- If feedback is not an issue, are you looking to use the single-channel communication systems of press advertising and television?

Creative scope

- Do you intend to choose a medium for its creative scope?

- If the message you are trying to get across is in itself quite mundane, do you think it might benefit from a quite novel or extraordinary approach?

Data availability

- Have you undertaken a comprehensive media buying operation despite the fact that the amounts of money to be spent are relatively small?

4. Other choices in media

- Have you considered the many other activities and channels available in addition to the mainstream media?

Note: Some of the alternative public relations activities and channels that can be considered are listed in Table 3, Step 6 of Part 1.

Having analyzed the choice of media available and the criteria for making your selection, the focus must now turn to good media relations and the value of editorial publicity. Extensive information for this is provided in Step 7 of Part 1. A brief list of appropriate audit questions follows an outline of this step.

GOOD MEDIA RELATIONS

BACKGROUND INFORMATION

The value of good editorial publicity is often as great as any other message source if not greater. It is also probably the most cost-effective channel of communication and so should be utilized as much as possible.

As a result of its value, journalists are swamped by information from all types of organization. Whether these companies get the publicity they want in terms of accuracy and positive tone depends on the goodwill of the journalists involved and how well those journalists are informed. Endeavoring to establish good working relationships with journalists will increase the chance that your press release will stand out from the many others and that a journalist may come to you for a comment on some industry issue.

In looking at editorial publicity, there are four key issues to be considered.

1. Guidelines on news releases.

2. What makes news?

3. Press receptions.

4. Press visits.

In the "Questions" section below you will find a set of questions that will help you to examine each of these issues.

QUESTIONS

• Have you put together a list of media whose support might be critical to your organization's success?

• Have you instigated a program of making the acquaintance of the key journalists and maintaining these relationships?

1. Guidelines on news releases

• In looking at your news releases, are they:

  ❏ between 100 and 300 words

  ❏ written in the same style as the journalist would write it

❏ written in a factual, authoritative manner

❏ lively and interesting

❏ written with no trace of a hard sell?

- Is the important news at the top of the news release and the supporting information further down?

The following aspects of news release writing should be borne in mind:

- structure

- headline

- first paragraph

- second and third paragraphs

- fourth paragraph

- fifth paragraph, and

- further information.

Structure

- Do your news releases have beginnings, middles, and ends?

Headline

- Are your headlines attention-grabbing?

- Do they sum up the essential news in three or four words?

First paragraph

- Given the importance of the first paragraph, do yours contain the main news angle written from the reader's point of view?

Second and third paragraphs

- Do your second and third paragraphs elaborate on the main story already told in the first paragraph?

- Do they only give the highlights of what you are trying to put across?

Fourth paragraph

- Have you put in a quote from someone in authority (and preferably outside the organization)?

Fifth paragraph

- Have you included facts and data in the fifth paragraph (e.g. price, delivery, date of an event)?

Further information

- Have you provided two names that can be contacted, with both office and home telephone and fax numbers?

- In writing your news release, have you also:
  - ❏ kept sentences short
  - ❏ avoided jargon and abbreviations
  - ❏ ensured a clear, attractive layout
  - ❏ typed on one side only with double-spacing and wide margins
  - ❏ sent the release only to media that will find it interesting
  - ❏ used a photograph wherever possible
  - ❏ captioned the photograph
  - ❏ put any amplification of the story on a separate sheet of a different color, or in an accompanying publication
  - ❏ asked journalists to criticize your new releases
  - ❏ written 'more follows' at the bottom of the first page and 'ends' at the end
  - ❏ included the date of the release and an embargo if there is one
  - ❏ included contact names and details
  - ❏ kept to short paragraphs (40 words or so)
  - ❏ avoided superlatives and exaggerated claims
  - ❏ written in the style of the publication?

2. *What makes news?*

- Have you made an assessment of what makes news according to your company?

Note: A checklist of 20 newsworthy topics is given in Table 4, Step 7 of Part 1. To this checklist should be added specialized company topics.

- Have you considered producing video and audiotape news releases for television networks and radio stations?

- Have you checked whether the publishing of editorial material depends on the placement of some supporting advertising?

Note: This is to be avoided as far as possible because the quality of a publication cannot be considered very high if the criterion for editorial inclusion is the size of your advertising budget as opposed to the intrinsic value of the news.

3. Press receptions

- Are you aware that, generally, there are too many of these and the press do not like them?

- Have you considered a press reception because of one of the following valid reasons:
  ❏ the item of news is really important to the medium concerned
  ❏ there is a need for questions to be asked and answered
  ❏ there needs to be a product demonstration
  ❏ there needs to be a number of one-to-one interviews?

4. Press visits

- Are you aware that, generally, journalists like press visits?

- Have you considered the importance of such an event being well done and the journalists well looked after?

- As the result of a press visit, are you anticipating:
  ❏ good, well-informed coverage
  ❏ the cementing of relationships for other times and events?

Having explored the importance of editorial publicity and how to produce a good news release, we now need to look at how to evaluate public relations. Information for this is provided in Step 8 of Part 1. A brief list of appropriate audit questions follows an outline of this step.

PUBLIC RELATIONS
EVALUATION

BACKGROUND INFORMATION

The starting point for any public relations evaluation has to be the strategic objectives of corporate image. Once these have been measured and tracked, the next stage is to assess how well each of the component parts of the media mix is succeeding.

In the "Questions" section below you will find the key questions to ask when carrying out an evaluation of public relations.

QUESTIONS

- Have you got some strategic objectives for your organization's corporate image?

- Were these objectives quantified initially?

- Are you now able to measure and track their progress?

- Are you able to assess editorial publicity and all the other media channels that you are utilizing against a number of set criteria (e.g. number of press cuttings, number of inquiries, number of visitors to road shows or exhibitions)?

Note: A checklist of typical communications channels and some suggested criteria for their evaluation is provided in Table 5, Step 8 of Part 1.

- Will the evaluation be carried out in-house or will you require some outside research assistance?

Having thought through your public relations evaluation procedure, we move on to a 10-point public relations action plan. Full details for this are provided in Step 9 of Part 1. A brief list of appropriate audit questions follows an outline of this step.

THE TEN-POINT PUBLIC RELATIONS PLAN

BACKGROUND INFORMATION

A public relations plan can be broken down into 10 separate steps. It is arguable that the first step should be research and not objectives if information for compiling the plan is not available. If it is available, the 10 steps of the plan can consist of the following.

Step One – Objectives.

Step Two – Issues.

Step Three – Strategy.

Step Four – Audiences (External and Internal).

Step Five – Messages.

Step Six – Media Plan.

Step Seven – Timetable.

Step Eight – Budget.

Step Nine – Measurement.

Step Ten – Resources.

In the "Questions" section below you will find a set of questions that will take you through these different steps.

QUESTIONS

Step One – Objectives

- Have you put together a clear statement of the aims of the plan, taking into account the business objectives?

- Are these objectives simple to understand, unambiguous and, most importantly, quantified?

Step Two – Issues

- Have you assessed whether or not there are any internal or external issues that could undermine the achievement of these objectives?

- If there are some issues that could have this effect, have you changed the objectives appropriately?

Step Three – Strategy

- Have you set down how you aim to achieve the objectives?

Step Four – Audiences (External and Internal)

- In order to achieve the greatest cost-effectiveness for your public relations campaign, have you carried out the following two essential activities:
  - ❏ fine tuned each of the publics into narrow groups with the same homogeneous characteristics
  - ❏ quantified the people concerned (internal and external)?

Note: In industrial or business markets, fine tuning each of the publics means identifying the people in the decision-making units (DMUs) and not just the organizations.

Step Five – Messages

- Have you identified the benefits of the product or service you are publicizing?

- Are any of these perceived benefits as opposed to actual benefits?

- Are your messages transmitted as the requirements of a prospect?

- Are your messages prioritized and tailored to fit each person in the DMU?

Step Six – Media Plan

- As the channels of communication through which the messages are sent to the target audience, does your plan show how each of the components relates to the others in terms of time, messages and corporate identity?

- Have the channels of communication been matched to each of the target audiences for minimum wastage?

- Have you also remembered media for the internal market?

Step Seven – Timetable

- On what scale has the timetable been set?

THE PUBLIC RELATIONS AUDIT

- Is the timetable on a rolling basis?

- Are you using a Gantt chart and making provision for periodic reviews?

Step Eight – Budget

- Has a budget been set?

- Is this budget the result of working through each of the steps, having a regard for the task to be achieved, and costing all the various items built into the plan?

Step Nine – Measurement

- Are you clear about the importance of campaign evaluation?

- Will you be carrying out some kind of tracking in order to make adjustments to the campaign if targets are not being met?

Step Ten – Resources

- Have you included in the plan:
  - ❏ the number of people to be involved in implementing the campaign
  - ❏ their professional capability to carry out the work involved with maximum efficiency?

- Do you need to include the use of outside services such as a public relations consultancy?

- Do you need to mention training needs and expenses?

In addition to the above ten points, the following items may need to be considered:
- introduction
- research
- quantifying
- media plan
- budgets
- executive summary, and
- tables and charts.

Introduction

- In any background notes, do you need to include internal and external factors such as PEEST (political, economic, environmental, sociological, technological) and SWOT (strengths, weaknesses, opportunities, threats)?

Research

- If any essential factors are unknown, have you made provision for initial research over and above what will be conducted at the evaluation stage?

Quantifying

- Do you need to pay particular attention to quantifying objectives and target audiences as well as a media breakdown?

Media plan

- Does the media plan represent the main body of the report?

- Does it list the media in detail and provide the rationale for using those chosen and why others were rejected?

Budgets

- Are the budgets task oriented and bottom up rather than top down?

- Are the actual media to be used indicated?

Executive summary

- Have you included an executive summary at the beginning or the end of the report as a short summary of the proposed actions and the reasons behind them?

Tables and charts

- Have these been used wherever possible?

CONCLUSION

Hopefully all of the questions listed in this section will help you to plan a public relations audit to ensure you are successfully establishing, maintaining and enhancing the reputation of your organization. The extensive explanations in Part 1 will help you to answer these questions to best effect.

Part 1: **Norman Hart** *MSc FCAM FIPR FCIM is currently Managing Director of Norman Hart Associates, a marketing and training consultancy based in Tunbridge Wells, UK, where he specializes in marketing communications. He has been a publicity manager with AEI, a publisher with Morgan-Grampian, and a marketing manager with Unilever. He is the author of numerous books including* Industrial Marketing Communications, Strategic Public Relations, *and* The Marketing Dictionary. *He is a Visiting Fellow of both Bradford and Leeds Universities, a Course Director at the College of the Chartered Institute of Marketing, and currently teaches the PR elective on the Hull Business School MBA. Mr Hart is Chairman of the International Public Relations Foundation. Part 2 has been adapted from* The Company AuditGuide *published by Cambridge Strategy Publications Ltd. Part 3 has been developed by Cambridge Strategy Publications Ltd.*